THE ANTI-WISDOM MANUAL

THE ANTI-WISDOM MANUAL

A Practical Guide to Spiritual Bankruptcy

Gilles Farcet, Ph.D.
Translated from the French by Mary Lyons

HOHM PRESS
Prescott, Arizona

Cover design: Kim Johansen
Layout and design: Bhadra Mitchell

Library of Congress Cataloging-in-Publication Data

Farcet, Gilles, 1959-
  [Manuel de l'anti sagesse. English]
  The anti-wisdom manual : a practical guide to spiritual bankruptcy / by Gilles Farcet ; translated from the French by Mary Lyons.
      p. cm.
  Includes bibliographical references and index.
  ISBN 1-890772-42-9 (alk. paper)
1. Religion--Controversial literature. I. Title.
  BL2775.3.F3713 2004
  204--dc22

                                        2004026090

HOHM PRESS
P.O. Box 2501
Prescott, AZ 86302
800-381-2700
http://www.hohmpress.com

This book was printed in the U.S.A. on acid-free paper using soy ink.

08 07 06 05   5 4 3 2 1

The true friend helps you take the full measure
of your enemy.
– Iranian proverb

Errare humanum est, perseverare diabolicum.
– Latin proverb

Any resemblance to egos, alive or deceased,
is purely intentional.

CONTENTS

FOREWORD

by Stephen Jourdain
author of *Radical Awakening*

Gilles,

Of course, I have always known you to be wholly built upon that tiny ocean of pure life people used to call "a soul" – I find proper to approach it with words such as "innocence," "childhood," "poetry." And here I am, reading the first pages of your *Anti-Wisdom Manual* ... Amazement and wonder overwhelm me: you dared!

Gilles, my friend, my brother, you dared! Innocence does not incline to war; but when it finds itself confronted with its mortal foe, that spiritual moisture which is indulgence in preconceived ideas and conventional feeling, acquiescence to sloppy consensus and intellectual fashion – be it imported from the East – and to its cheap "me," then innocence must, like the musketeer, draw its sword and strike. The sword of innocence, your sword, Gilles, is that of satire and mockery, but, let there be no confusion here, you are not using it to hurt or harm, you seize it to save and heal. I'll end with this remark: it seems to me that, the subversive enterprise which is your book, is, as far as the spiritual field is concerned, the first of its kind, a world premiere.

INTRODUCTION

Certain traditional teachings give preference to the so-called negative approach: rather than try to say what God or the Absolute *is*, one formulates everything *they are not*.

This manner of attacking things sometimes proves very efficient, to the extent that it isn't a question of trying to make the light burst forth but of dissipating the darkness, to affirm the truth rather than flush out the error that obscures it for us.

Modestly written along these lines, this little book proposes to transmit a bit of the practice of the Way by exposing the axis of non-practice.

Among the authors of works dubbed "spiritual," let's admit it, many have only a partial experience of what they're declaring. The author of *The Anti-Wisdom Manual*, otherwise known as the Spiritual Enemy, can, on the other hand, claim an experience that is perfectly first-hand.

Assisting to the best of his ability a well-known French spiritual master, he has had, over the last twenty years, many occasions to experiment with the twists and turns of non-practice, the doubtful delights of recuperation by the ego and the mind from the most profound teachings, the pitfalls of the relationship with the Spiritual Friend, and the entire gamut of perversities that exist daily in spiritual retreats, monasteries, ashrams and other centers dedicated to the essential.

Thus he only had to dip into his own past to write what follows.

Other than the memory of his own errors past and present, the author also found material in his daily encounters with other people's aberrations, which his function as an instructor of the Way has presented to him.

It's true that error has this peculiarity – that it is, all things considered, nothing personal. Repeated in all its forms from one generation to the next, circulating from monastery to ashram, from school to center, from disciple to seeker, it's like a singular virus diffused among a multitude of individual organisms, each one eroded from within by the same infection, each one having to deal with his own malady. The errors, perversities and caricatures exposed here are those of the ego and mind, in other words, those of each and every one of us.

Let everyone, therefore, consider himself concerned; let no one, however, take offense.

Talking about the unawakened human condition, Mr. Gurdjieff [1] spoke of the "horror of the situation." This *Anti-Wisdom Manual* will begin, let's hope, by making one smile. From smiling, perhaps one will proceed to a certain seriousness, the one that is indispensable to truly starting on the Way.

In other words, this guide could be entitled: *How to Sin While Pretending to Find One's Salvation*. Let he or she who is without sin cast the first stone.

Author's Note to The Reader

The Anti-Wisdom Manual is, in great part, intended to be a rigorous exposé, though from the negative point of view, of a specific path – that transmitted by Arnaud Desjardins [2] and inherited from Swami Prajnanpad. [3]

I am imbued – even if still not enough – by this path both in my private life as a student and in the weave, so to speak, of my professional activities as one of the collaborators of Arnaud Desjardins, since 1996, at the Hauteville Ashram, where I am charged in this capacity with transmitting the teaching at his side, under his benevolent guidance and in the limits of my abilities.

Unable and unwilling to escape being imbued, early on I decided, while editing this present work, not to erase or limit my use of specific references to the teachings of Arnaud Desjardins.

A similar attempt, *a priori* justifiable, desirable even where universality is concerned, quickly seemed artificial and, moreover, useless to me.

In effect, whatever the particularities in terminology as well as in method of every path worthy of its name may be, each one is essentially *The* Path. Just as Arnaud Desjardins' books are not addressed exclusively to his students, I dare wish that this book, given its modest level, could speak to every person who feels concerned by "the path and its pitfalls."

After all, the subject of each chapter – that is: the relationship to the spiritual master; vigilance; mastering the thoughts; intimate relationships; managing emotions; and non-duality – are not only not the exclusive domain of any particular Way, but are common to all. Moreover, if no school or tradition has a monopoly on the truth, neither does any one have the monopoly on error. For error is precisely the topic here with the intention that it acts as a mirror for the truth.

Lastly, let it be clear that I alone am responsible for the contents of this *Anti-Wisdom Manual*. The limitations of the book are mine; what truth it carries does not belong to me.

---

[1]George Gurdjieff (1874-1949) – an Armenian-born spiritual teacher and author whose teachings – known as "The Fourth Way" – are aimed at awakening humans from the "sleep" of their conditioning.

[2]Arnaud Desjardins (born 1925) – a contemporary spiritual teacher and author, formerly a respected French film-maker, based in southern France. Arnaud carries on the teaching of his eminent Indian guru, Swami Prajnanpad.

[3]Swami Prajnanpad (1891-1974) – a highly-educated Indian college professor with a compelling passion for the truth. He became a respected guru, and taught a way called "adyatma yoga," integrating the most profound spiritual principles with everyday life.

If You Run Into Buddha, Don't Say Hi

How to Avoid and Annul the Master-Disciple Relationship

*You can't follow the master,
but you can imitate him.*
- The Spiritual Enemy

First and foremost take note: your Spiritual Enemy can't warn you enough on this most delicate point. All traditions without exception have stressed the fundamental nature of the master-disciple relationship. The success of your mission to sabotage it therefore depends, in great part, on avoiding this universal and immemorial plague that is the spiritual master.

Luckily, ambient confusion in no way facilitates a simple and rational approach to this question. The discredit attached to all forms of authority, from the primal parental authority to that of the highest levels of government, the reign of rampant individualism, the media coverage of dangerous cults, the ascension of fundamentalism, the emergence of *new age* ideology, the loss of respect for the manual arts that goes hand in hand with the disappearance of our very notion of apprenticeship, the loss of meaning as to what is sacred ... so many factors that conveniently cloud the issue and guarantee an approach to the question that is, *a priori*, wrong. Add to that the proliferation of pseudo "enlightened ones," the rarity today, as yesterday, of authentic spiritual masters as well as disciples, and you'll fully realize just how little risk there is. Nevertheless, *one well-advised anti-*

practitioner is worth two. Despite the accumulation of conditions capable of nipping any passing fancy about establishing a relationship with the master in the bud, it would be naïve to underestimate the potential menace.

Never forget that even excluded, unknown, mocked, exiled or ill, a spiritual master conserves terrifying powers of benevolence and a blessing power capable of infiltrating the zones one thought were the best protected. Your Spiritual Enemy therefore recommends that you take careful precautions against that contamination, keeping in mind that with a master there is always a degree of risk.

To guarantee the failure of your spiritual practice while of course pretending to pursue it, the simplest and most effective method is to avoid, *a priori* and on principle, any contact with a living master. With that end in mind, several strategies can be considered.

A Good Master is a Dead Master

Proclaim yourself the disciple of a deceased master with whom you feel particularly "in touch." Preferably choose a really famous master with universal recognition. If, for example, a photo of Ananda Mayi Ma[1] makes your heart beat faster, decide immediately that, based on the emotion you feel, she is your master and guides you from the next world. If mystical transports and inspiration from the other side aren't your cup of tea, decide, on the basis of your intellectual interest in the words and letters of Swami Prajnanpad, that you are his direct disciple. To reinforce your position, studiously avoid the master's actual students, especially Arnaud Desjardins who is particularly harmful because he was authorized to teach by Swami Prajnanpad himself. Take care to imply that you prefer to drink directly from the source, continually praise the "purity" and "radicality" of Swamiji and glance condescendingly at Desjardins and his own students.

Here's another possibility: declare yourself the disciple of Ramana Maharshi, practicing the direct method of "Who Am I?" or, alternatively, that you are the heir of Nisargadatta Maharaj at the peak of non-duality having, thus, long ago gone beyond the illusion of relationship.

Once again, the essential thing is to avoid all contact with a living master. That way you will never risk really being taken to task for the way you function. The master will remain that flattering reference who will intervene for you whenever you wish and who can be pushed aside when that best suits you.

Show great esteem for the "inner teacher." All the spiritual teachings and most of the masters themselves have insisted on the importance of access to the "inner guru." Make these words, easily found in a number of books, your own and apply them to your current level; claim to be able to completely and immediately forego every "exterior" master. After that you can convincingly rationalize your position at leisure by detouring around the indisputable truths. For example, wherever you go, repeat these words, "Life is the greatest master." Or if you prefer, "One can learn so much from children or, for that matter, anyone encountered along the way." No one will be able to contradict you and therefore your mind will be at ease.

To reinforce your position, abridge quotations. For example, quote the phrase of Swami Prajnanpad, "Swamiji has no disciples," while carefully avoiding to mention the rest, "Swamiji has only candidates to discipleship."

In this way you will manage to give that formula a meaning exactly opposite to Swamiji's proposal. Quoted from start to finish, the formula presents becoming a disciple as the accomplishment, the goal. Half-quoted, it suggests the opposite.

Generally, a quotation that's been abridged or taken out of context constitutes a very effective weapon that you can use without stinting, following in this process the example of the master of us all, the devil, who in order to tempt Christ once used this shrewd method – check the Gospel where Satan quotes the Scriptures in order to convince Christ to deny himself. Don't let Satan's failure discourage you. That doesn't change the fact that he's the prince of the world. And then, it's yourself first and foremost that you need to dupe.

Along the same lines, unabashedly make use of the famous formula: "If you run into Buddha, kill him." Emphasize the murder, hush up the encounter. Some good advice: Don't even expose yourself to the remotest risk of making Buddha's – that's to say a living master's – acquaintance. Kill him right away, preferably from a safe distance. Generally speaking it's

---

[1]A short description of the teachers and spiritual masters noted in this chapter can be found in Appendix A.

always handy to memorize a few "shock," rather than "stock," phrases requiring a high level of spiritual development – and only comprehensible to that level – and then apply them to the context of everyday psychology. A perversion that's proven its worth.

In order to feed your argument against the rapport between master and disciple, base it on two to three postulates, always the same, pertaining to that relationship; little does it matter that these postulates are false and actually the exact opposite of reality. In fact it's essential that they're completely untenable so that you can easily denounce their inanity. Here are the postulates:

★ The master claims to possess the truth.
★ It's a question of venerating the person of the master considered as a human being in and of himself more worthy of consideration than anyone else.
★ Therefore, the master encourages and supports the childish transfer to his person.

Above all, don't push intellectual honesty to the point of taking the trouble to explore the veracity of these postulates. Consider them as givens and base your arguments on them. Any sensible, well-disposed person will necessarily take your side when you denounce these dangerous absurdities.

See the exception as the rule. Ramana Maharshi, Ananda Mayi Ma didn't have flesh and blood masters. Do as they did, on this point only of course. The fact that they led lives of asceticism and total surrender is only a secondary consideration.

Along the same lines, find the special cases – the phenomenons, the misfits – wonderfully exciting. Only swear by that licentious and debauched Tibetan monk, forget all the Rinpoches who've led virtuous lives. Make little of the actual Dalai Lama, much too nice and conventional – doesn't he go so far as to say that first and foremost he's a Buddhist monk? – and focus your interest exclusively on the sixth Dalai Lama, a skirt-chaser who died poisoned. Now that's more original and will provide a cut-rate security deposit against all your emotional attachments and weaknesses. There's no greater boon to the Spiritual Enemy than a master who is not only dead but also a bad example.

Become a krishnamurtian – and by the same stroke

insult the memory of Krishnamurti – like people used to become communists. As soon as you hear the word "master," whip out your doctrinal revolver – under the circumstances, a quotation from the great man. Since no one can deny his importance you will be unattackable. Above all, carefully pass over any mention of the worship of which Krishnamurti was and still is the object.

Once and for all, and with no concessions, adopt the ultimate and non-dualistic perspective: There is no one; psychology doesn't exist; there is neither master nor disciple; and, while we're at it, who's asking the question? Your immunity will thus resist everything.

Little does it matter that there is indeed "someone" each time you are swept away by an emotion or an ordinary desire. The important thing is to repeat with sufficient authority that there is "no one." Used consistently, this tactic can quite quickly lead you to a robotic state where your merest sentiment will be run through the non-dualist meat grinder.

Whereas it will be necessary for you to avoid disciples with a high degree of advancement as well as the masters, on the other hand you have the advantage of being able to frequent the novice or less diligent disciples. Their childishness, their naiveté and fanatical or insipid devotion will reinforce your position.

For good measure check out the "seniors" as well. Just as churches have their holier-than-thou parishioners, the monasteries their grumpy brothers or moustached, pinch-lipped sisters, every spiritual community or *sangha* has its contingent of rather paltry "seniors." It could be that their sad appearance hides real qualities, but appearances, of course, will be the only thing you trust. What's essential is that there's nothing enviable about them. When you first make contact with a spiritual community, whichever one it is, concentrate on the pettiness, the intrigues, the jealousies. You'll always find such things and that can't help but confirm your beliefs.

Beware of the Guru

If you do take the risk of approaching spiritual instructors despite these recommendations, never frequent masters entrenched in a tradition who refer to their own master as well as to a lineage; choose the self-proclaimed "enlightened ones." You'll have no trouble finding them, they spring up just about everywhere like weeds. You'll be able to recognize them from the way they make it a point of honor that they've never been disciples nor do they have disciples – without that stopping them from letting a band of admirers and zealots come their way. Indeed, this new style of instructor doesn't have disciples – what a horrid word! – he has "friends." Rather than a "structure" or "organization" he has a website that informs his "friends" of each of his appearances. Become one of his many "friends." There's no obligation and it's a nice thing to do.

All these recommendations should allow you to escape, head held high, from the attraction of the master.

Nevertheless, your Spiritual Enemy owes it to himself to accompany you in any situation, even the worst as regards your non-progression along the road.

Let's say that, despite all the strategies proposed above, you succumb to the blessing power of an authentic, living master. Don't despair. Your mind has indeed lost a battle but not the war.

Be assured that there is no menace that the ego can't convert to an advantage. Examples abound of sincere seekers having succeeded, in spite of regular contact with one or more sages, in sabotaging their path or *sadhana*.

Here are several suggestions for getting yourself out of a tight spot.

First and foremost, follow the *principle of dispersion*. If you really must expose yourself to wisdom in the flesh, don't limit yourself to assiduously frequenting one particular sage; that would lead to the dire risk of a commitment. On the contrary, cultivate relationships, as friendly as they are superficial, with as many masters as possible. Collect masters the way Don Juan collected mistresses. A master is dangerous above all because of the immediate and subtle influence (the famous *baraka*) he exercises naturally on those who approach him. The surest way of counteracting an influence is to expose yourself to multiple influences before one among them can begin to take root in you.

Therefore, become a tourist of the essential. Run from ashram to center to monastery. "Welcome everywhere, committed nowhere" – that must be your motto. Compile initiations, benedictions and lessons. Take refuge with the Tibetans, practice zazen every once in a while, be baptized by an orthodox priest, dance around the fire with a shaman, hang out on the fringe of a group of Sufis, receive the silent blessing of Chandra Swami, snuggle in the embrace of Ammachi once or twice a year – even take advantage of the moment to ask her for a mantra that you'll occasionally remember. Go to Ramesh Balsekar in Bombay and nod approvingly whenever he tells you that everything "just happens."

It would be a shame to leave out the Western instructors. Therefore, take a training course with Richard Moss, go on retreat with Andrew Cohen, be a Gurdjieff groupie ... Do a little work on *hara* with Karlfried Graf Dürckeim's successsor, Jacques Castermane in France – but not too much – just enough to bolster your ego, not enough to make it feel uneasy, then decide that if only you'd gotten to know Dürckheim himself ... As far as Lee Lozowick is concerned, content yourself with a single public lecture – he'll be part of your personal hit-parade that way – but avoid the seminars. He is so insistent on the importance not only of the master but of one master that you risk coming out of there badly shaken. Get decapitated by Douglas Harding, from time to time; have a dizzying conversation with the author of *Radical Awakening*, Stephen Jourdain; then go take a few days' rest at Arnaud Desjardins' ashram in the south of France. By the way, that ashram is just a few miles away from Castermane's place, so that makes it ideal for a tour of the French Spiritual sights. Though Desjardins himself and his close disciples are rather tough practitioners, they tend to be very benevolent towards anyone who wants to just hang around a few days, provided you behave nicely. You therefore may feel safe going there. Returning, however, may prove more dangerous, so take heed.

Ask all these eminent people the very same questions. Pinpointing the contradictions as well as the incompatibilities in their respective responses will thus be child's play. Become familiar with all these precepts without really knowing any one of them. This spiritual channel-flipping will provide a unique opportunity to travel around the world and meet some nice people. If anyone accuses you of dispersion, the obvious reply is that all roads lead to the same goal, that all masters transmit the same message and that you have a horror of fanaticism. You can also deftly play on the confusion of levels: hide behind the example of well-known masters or disciples who themselves have frequented hordes of sages and instructors aside from their own "Spiritual Friend" – your departure point being that what applied to them (longtime practitioners of a way that has taken root in them and for which any new contact is a confirmation) applies equally to you, that creaking ship set rocking by the merest breeze.

If, devil forbid, the principle of dispersion hasn't been respected and you've unfortunately taken it into your head to attach yourself to one particular way with one particular master, all is not lost as long as you take advantage of the following advice: come to the master not as a student or apprentice but as a patient. Go on and on about your divorce, your love life, your various and diverse frustrations, the difficulties your children cause you, your boss, your neighbor, being careful to only approach these concerns in a linear manner. Complain, whimper, present yourself as a victim and expect, without actually believing it, that the master will work a miracle for you. Don't consider even for a second the possibility of seriously putting the teachings into practice. Reduce practice to a few hollow formulas such as, "I must say yes," "I've got to let go," "I have to surrender" – formulas to which you'll systemically add, "but I can't."

Turn the master into a psychoanalyst, a financial or marriage counselor, a sexologist, or even a witch doctor ... anything except a spiritual master who is inviting you to change levels. Since the master is none of the above, you can't miss being disappointed. Refer everything back not just to psychology but to pop psychology.

I'm as Disciple as They Get

If you find the strategy of the "patient" unflattering to the ego, you can always resort to the tactic called the "great disciple" or "I'm as disciple as they get."

Proceed in a fashion exactly opposite to that of the patient strategy in order to arrive at the same result. Reject all psychology, especially if it's seen from the perspective of awakening. If anyone dares tell you that you might perhaps consider undergoing therapy or some kind of work on the unconscious, laugh in his face. Never undertake anything the least bit personal. From the teachings, only retain the ultimate, impersonal, beyond-the-beyond-of-beyond perspective. Ask only metaphysical questions about the One, the All, non-separation, taking care to make these questions as abstract as possible. You can risk manipulating the most elevated ideas as long as you never relate them to the merest concrete aspect of your existence. For example, criticize non-separation and non-duality while forgetting you're at drawn daggers with your ex-husband or mother-in-law. Under every circumstance adopt the attitude of the "senior" for whom everything is crystal clear. Implicitly reproach the master and his entourage for making far too many concessions to psychology.

Take care never to enter into a relationship with "the" master, but always with "your" master – he of your fantasies, your desires and your fears.

Seek not to be wise but to appear wise. Don't follow the master, imitate him.

Adopt his intonations, mimic his gestures, copy his posture. If you're a fan of zen, laugh loudly, gulp down sake, inappropriately quote obscure koans. Of course this is just an example, you're free to perfect and put the finishing touches on your own imitations.

Sport spectacles and become the sangha nerd. Make sure each phrase, pronounced in sententious tones, begins with: "The master (Swamiji, guruji, Baba, Rinpoche, Bhagavan, Sensei, His Holiness, Sidi Sheik, Arnaud, Lee – the choice is yours) said that … " or better yet, " … told me that … "

When you approach the master, always adopt a twisted disposition. You have a choice between two attitudes, seemingly contradictory but equally effective: dripping devotion or crude casualness. Choose one or the other depending on your natural inclinations.

If you're inclined to *dripping devotion*, childishness must dominate in your relationship with the master. Make every effort to justify, through your actions, the criticism of those who only see regression and neurosis in the master-disciple relationship. Be a caricature of a disciple, a gurufied creature.

When in the presence of the master take care that your comportment is gauche, exempt of anything natural. Be servile, obsequious, uselessly attentive. Confuse respect with idolatry. Under the pretext of "devotion," deify the person of the master.

Provide him with a halo. Never imagine he might also be a human being. That way you'll be thrown off balance each time you surprise him picking his nose or spilling food on his sweater.

Staunchly maintain the idea that you have a particular, special, romantic relationship with him. Start from the principle that the master loves everyone, but you more than the others. If, while meditating, he stares straight ahead, it's certainly you his eyes are fixed upon. If he proffers a few generalities about the sacred intimacy of the master-disciple relationship, it's about your relationship with him he's talking about in veiled phrases. Make cow eyes at him. Lovers are always alone in this world ... Permanently fix your gaze of enamored, devoted beatitude on him. Pronounce his name at every opportunity, your voice quivering with emotion.

If the master is a married man or living with someone and you're a woman, decide that his mate isn't good enough for him, that he stays with her out of compassion and a sense of duty, but that you would be much better able to look after him ... Thus entertain the hope of a separation followed by your enthronement as "Mother" or, even more exciting, hope for a "tantric" and secret relationship with the guru – at least at the beginning – before you think about making your situation official once the time for fooling around is over.

Stalk him. If he takes the same route at the same time every day, post yourself along the way where you're sure he'll see you. If you find yourself in his presence along with a few other people in an informal setting (a picnic, a stroll, a party), hover around him like a bird of prey, keep your eyes open looking for the crack you can slip between, and, as soon as you're where he can see you and he notices you, speak to him ... It goes without saying that you'll never dream of giving him a moment's peace.

Beg for his attention constantly. Implore a smile, a look, a word. The important thing is not to become an adult, liberated from the opinion of others, including the master's, but that you feel recognized, preferred, special. This childish positioning presents, among other things, the opportunity to consider everyone else as an opponent who you can look upon with false fraternity.

To take the logic as far as it will go: turn the master into a king, with the ashram ... the center ... the community, as his court. Your constant objective, like any conscientious courtesan's, is to be – or rather appear to be – close to the monarch. Secretly envy those who seem to enjoy his favor. Look daggers at those whom he invites to his table or with whom he speaks for more than thirty seconds. Intrigue, maneuver, push and shove.

If dripping devotion inspires your scorn, opt for *crude casualness*. Start with the exactly opposite principle: as much as the preceding point of view requires making marvels out of mole hills, this strategy requires that you render everything common, degrade it, take it for granted, until the ordinary becomes the mediocre.

As always, base your strategy on an undeniable truth ("after all, master or not, he's a human being"), which you are going to delightfully pervert by making assumptions based on preconceived ideas and by isolating this truth from the perspective of the whole.

Based on the strength of this "truth," be sure not to show any particular deference toward the master. Avoid the merest exterior sign of respect. That shouldn't be too hard. Our society, where courtesy is disappearing and bad manners are becoming the norm, has magnificently prepared you for that casualness which is confused with being oneself. Therefore, behave towards the master as you would with anyone else. When in the presence of the Spiritual Friend, banish any idea of protocol or politeness. Speak to him as you would to your college roommate, interrupt him, cut in front of him, never hold the door for him, begin to eat before he does, finish after him. When you're waiting for him to arrive for a teaching session, rather than using the time to reflect, talk loudly. Look condescendingly on all those who show respect. Congratulate yourself every instant for not being like the other poor slobs shackled by slavish devotion.

When I Grow Up, I'm Going to Be a Guru

Dripping devotion or crude casualness are only crutches, precious certainly, but you need to go beyond them in order to dig more deeply and rot the relationship at the core.

To assure that the worm enters the apple, the basic axiom is the following: albeit "more advanced," "highly evolved," "awakened," "realized," "enlightened," etc., the master is (in the final analysis) "just like me." Don't see him as a human being free of ego, see him as a free ego. A free ego envied, admired, favored ... in brief, the incarnation, not of possible freedom, but of perfect ambition. Think of the master as delivered from "suffering" without envisioning that he might also be delivered from "happiness."

Consequently, when you enter into contact with the Spiritual Friend make sure that right away it's with the intention of becoming not a disciple but a master. In more common terms, you need to goof things up by alleging to accede to the position of guru.

The master seen as a free ego is an ideal version of the ME. Take that axiom to its limit and opt for the strategy of *fusional consensus*. The master is a great master because he thinks as I do. He is the champion of my ideology, the emblem of my vision of the world. He expresses what I feel, defends what I believe in. He is the sublime and definitive confirmation of everything I represent and hope for.

With regard to the master, fusional consensus leads you to adopt a position identical to that which is dominant at the beginning of an infatuation: s/he – that magnificent other unlike anyone else – is the key to paradise, my other half, my soul mate, the missing piece, the answer to my prayers, a marvelous mirror telling me I'm the most beautiful of all. Sooner or later, and according to a well-known itinerary, that idyllic phase will inevitably give way to a period of doubt and uneasiness: in the end, s/he doesn't think exactly like me; s/he is not absolutely perfect, that's to say, the same as me.

In fact, the time will necessarily come when the master, if he's authentic, will disturb you ... run counter, more or less directly, to the way you regard yourself and the world. The moment has arrived to sabotage the relationship.

Yes, But ...

In order to do this, rather than break things off right away, your Spiritual Enemy suggests you employ certain wiles that will permit you to drag things out, to poison the atmosphere, to give the master and his entourage a hard time; eventually, and it is a bonus not to be ignored, to upset the other students.

The game, then, consists of claiming to remain a student of the master – for a while at least – as you create various fallback positions.

Start by establishing a clear distinction between the "divine," "impersonal" aspect of the master and his "human" aspect. This distinction, perfectly healthy and legitimate if it concerns noting that the master prefers one type of food to another, becomes marvelously pernicious the moment the "human" aspect is seen as interfering with the transmission itself.

The principle is simple: each time you have a bad reaction to something the Spiritual Friend has said or done or decided, see it as an expression of his human aspect. Tell yourself it's a question of background, of education, of generation ... Above all, don't speak to him about it, don't bring anything up directly: your doubts risk being cleared up, your uneasiness dissipated.

On the contrary, as soon as there's a doubt, a question, don't breathe a word. Outwardly demonstrate an infallible devotion; inwardly let your imagination run wild. You can even quite simply repress your doubts. They won't get the least bit lost. Be assured, they'll turn up when the moment is right to undermine your proceedings.

If it is strongly advised not to express your concerns and doubts directly to the master himself or to a member of his immediate entourage – who, having known and gone through periods of doubt might be capable of providing sound advice and perspective – on the other hand, don't hesitate to ask the advice of people as lacking in authority and as inexperienced as yourself. With a sure hand, the unconscious, an important ally of the Spiritual Enemy, will guide you to where others are feeling as ravaged (at the same time, by the same dissensions) as you. Stir each other up, launch yourselves in endless debate, buoy yourselves with false illusions, express your thoughts as one person, mutually support each other as you plot and scheme. Thick as thieves, you'll be all the stronger in legitimizing the barriers you've created, rationalizing what you've misunderstood, and thus sabotaging the opportunity of a, if not several, lifetimes.

Following that logic, incessantly measure the words and acts of the Spiritual Friend against the standards by which you yourself function. Since he's a human being "like you," he is, like you, capable of projecting, of identifying himself with, and thus of nourishing personal preferences, likes and dislikes, of cherishing his opinion, of feeling attacked and thus defending himself ... If he makes reference to his own experience past or present, he's manifesting self-satisfaction; if he remains sober and silent, he's cold and frigid. If he remarks on a specific trait in your behavior, seek to demonstrate your mind and the ego at work based on the examination of what you've done, written or said, and that that, quite naturally, unsettles you; above all, don't take the time to really listen and to assimilate his remark. Conclude immediately that he didn't understand you, that an aspect of the situation escapes him. Feel humiliated, hurt, outraged, unjustly treated. It's the moment to let all the little doubts buried inside you come out into the light of day.

Whatever he might say to you, reply either "no" or, more subtly, "yes, but … "

Don't pay the slightest attention to any of his eventual suggestions. If he advises you to practice some type of physical exercise, tell yourself he's "missed the boat," that that's not your cup of tea. If he advises you against a certain professional or emotional orientation, ignore it. Make a habit of presenting him with a done deed. Don't solicit his feelings on a matter, inform him of it once the decision has been made and put into action, when it's too late or too difficult to undo things. If he gives you the order to go back on your decision, accuse him of putting you in an impossible situation.

If, despite all the somber suggestions of your Spiritual Enemy, you're so stubborn that you can't yet bring yourself to erode the direct relationship with the master, the recourse of eroding the relationship with the ashram still remains.

My Little Grass Shack in Nirvana

Indeed, if, as is often the case, the master runs an ashram, the latter constitutes the concrete point of contact with the guru. Therefore, it's vital that your relationship with the ashram or community is as tainted as possible.

To this end, if you're a relative "newcomer," start out with the assumption that you've arrived too late. The master is too old, too busy … there are too many people … anyone and everyone is accepted … the seniors were lucky (you'll always find a few who will be delighted to back your opinion). Repeat to yourself that, if only you'd gotten to know the ashram and the master "at the beginning," today you would be well advanced in the way. Never mention the fact that, if certain seniors show proof of being truly experienced, many – the worthy disciples of the Spiritual Enemy – have given up or are foundering. Daydream of an ashram that you never knew, in order to get no benefit from the one that does exist and is available to you. You'll thus succeed in missing the real and present opportunity by replacing it with your image of an unreal opportunity that has already passed.

Cultivate not the beginner's spirit – fatal to non-practice – but the *winner's spirit*. Begin with the principle that you know all. Arrive at the ashram full of opinions, experiences and preconceived ideas. Incessantly compare the ashram you've found with your idea of what an ashram ought to be. Attach yourself firmly to this idea, support it with all the arrogance, pretension and obstinacy you can muster. A little persistence will show that, along this line, you can go far.

Taking the logic further, comport yourself at the ashram the way others comport themselves on a television talk show where the guest has been invited to defend his opinion tooth and nail. For you, the ashram should be a forum for debate and controversy. Be automatically "for" or "against" and justify this attitude by seeing it as the necessity to exercise your critical sense. If a rule or custom in usage at the ashram displeases you or even shocks you, react immediately. React immediately as well when something said during a group session or teaching goes against your own conceptions. Inopportunely intervene.

Don't ask, state. If you must formulate your intervention in terms of a question, do it only for form without bothering to wait for an eventual response. Don't take the time to think things over and understand. Declare yourself "astonished that … ," "surprised to observe that … " Drape yourself in virtuous indignation, well-founded suspicion, unshadowed doubt. In brief, you have no particular effort to put forth. At the ashram or center you merely have to be the way you are everywhere else, that's to say, on the defensive.

Don't arrive at the ashram or retreat center as a pupil but as a *paying guest*. Having taken the trouble to make the trip, you have *a right* to quality service. Consider that your visit is an honor; dispute, argue. Act as if the ashram owes you something, not the reverse. After all, aren't you the center of the universe?

Don't follow the rules and customs of the ashram or center

no matter what they might be. Act on the principle that these rules have nothing to do with your relationship – so beautiful, so pure, so sublime with the master, and that no one – especially not the master's entourage – could ever understand. Assign yourself the role of a fervent defender of the "spirit," opposed to the "letter" applied by a bunch of small-minded functionaries. Don't imagine for a second that it was the master himself who established these rules and feels it's important that they're followed. The less you respect the rules, the more you have to lay it on thick in your discourse on "devotion" and "commitment."

Some suggestions: Systematically arrive late – if only five minutes in order to demonstrate your sovereign independence – to all activities scheduled at a given hour. Talk while in the areas where and/or during the times in which one is expected to observe silence. Never make your bed. If you sleep in a dormitory or share a room, turn on the light in the middle of the night without taking into consideration that others are sleeping. Communal bathrooms equally offer marvelous opportunities to affirm your personality. After your ablutions, leave hair on the soap and a ring around everything. Let your little pals do the cleaning up.

Above all, neglect the details. Never push a chair back into place, never shut off a light, always slam the door …

An ashram or center is, in theory, a place of retreat. Therefore, take care to sabotage your own retreat by finding the merest pretext to leave the grounds. If the place is situated in proximity to a village, regularly go to the local coffee shop for a quick cup – in India, go to a tea shop – in order to release the tension created by an environment of reflection and silence, those indispensable ingredients of any retreat. That way, any possible benefit of your stay will be nipped in the bud. If anyone mentions this to you, immediately retort that there is no harm in leaving for fifteen minutes to take a coffee break and that the ashram is not a prison.

Along the same lines, you can spend your retreat glued to the phone. Rather than leaving your daily relations and occupations behind you for a while, maintain contact, remove any possibility to step back and reflect if only for a moment. To that end don't forget your cell phone. Check your messages every few hours, call home or, why not, your office daily. If, unfortunately, your ashram or center is located in some rural backwater where cell phones don't work, you can – at least in the Western Hemisphere – always track down a phone booth within a radius of a few miles. The inconvenience could turn out to be a plus in as far as it gives you a daily excuse to go out, to scatter your energies and possibly to skip some meditation sessions and other activities. Obviously, if anyone suggests you refrain from phoning, see that as an intolerable restriction to your personal freedom, a manipulation of your mind, the prelude to brainwashing and being cut off from the world, characteristic of cults. Consequently, don't compromise on this point. Being attached to the telephone is and must remain an individual's inalienable right.

Most ashrams and centers ask those on retreat to participate in daily chores, whether it's cooking, washing dishes, cleaning, gardening or odd jobs. Consider this aspect of communal life as completely beneath you. View the chores as an assortment of painful duties that have nothing to do with the reason you came. Consequently, declare yourself sick, tired, arthritic, unfit. If this strategy works you can take particular pleasure in reading a treatise on letting go and non-action while the others slave away. On the chance that those distributing the tasks can't be duped and you find yourself obliged to play the lackey, take care to botch the job. Resist, complain, dispatch your work in all haste. If the head of the cleaning crew gives you a hard time about an unemptied vacuum cleaner bag, that has nothing to do with your sadhana. It's him or her, as everyone knows, "that needs work."

If you're no longer a beginner in the matter of non-practice, you can benefit by applying the most perverse strategy, which consists of showing yourself willing to take the utmost care and concern to do a good job – as long as it's your idea. Begin by taking note of, if not the incompetence, at least the insufficiency of the people supervising the chores. From that point, short-circuit their instructions. Take initiative without being asked, contest all and any directives given down to the merest detail. If you are asked to cut the radishes in slices, dice them, if only on principle. If you work with a team, make sure your attitude of clear disapproval stirs up a hornet's nest. At the first remark of your group leader, label him or her as a narrow-minded, finicky functionary with whom any discussion is useless. Make sure to share your opinions with the others on retreat, especially the newest arrivals who are the easiest to influence. If, as is often the case in ashrams and monasteries, silence is requested during the work period, find any and every excuse to talk.

Finally, don't pass up the opportunity that work provides to grab hold of a little power. If it turns out you are competent and particularly effective in one realm or another, don't hesitate to make a big deal about it. The important thing is that everyone knows. Remember that your abilities are not to be used to serve the master and the ashram, but to serve your ego.

If, as with many ashrams with a certain reputation, the master is surrounded by assistants – swamis, devoted lamas, long-time disciples who have proven their worth – who act as intermediaries at his side, it is crucial that you avoid them. In reality, it could very well be that the realistic, non-fantasy access to the master depends on the clarity of your relationship with those bothersome second stringers. To be on bad terms with them guarantees you're being on bad terms with the master.

Don't confront them head on – that would be awkward and only too obvious. Tolerate their existence. When they give a teaching session, be sure to attend but without the slightest intention of listening to them. Deny them the right to teach or show you anything whatsoever. Don't forget that only the master is worthy of you. As soon as the others appear ... open their mouths ... make a gesture, compare them to the master, to their great disadvantage of course. Don't give them the slightest chance to be themselves with their own style and manner. Mentally comment and criticize the merest of their interventions. At each turn of phrase, behind each expression, discover their egos at work. List their weaknesses, errors, shortcomings. Make the radical and irrevocable distinction between them and the master – not considering the fact that they're only there and stay there because the master wishes it so.

If you can't completely duck those irritating supernumeraries in hopes of getting to the master, adopt a more insidious strategy: play them against each other. Ask one a question and the same question to another, and point out the differences in their approach. If there aren't any, invent one.

Divide up the pieces of the puzzle. Share a bit of information with one assistant, a confidence with another, a revelation to a third. For example, ask to speak with X and tell him about your wife – by the way, never be fully aware that when you talk about another person it's yourself that you reveal – but without mentioning you have a mistress. Then use whatever pretext is necessary to arrange to have a conversation with Y and tell him about the mistress. As a final step write to Z in the strictest confidence in order to confess to him, and him alone, that you and yet another mistress have a child no one else knows about. From start to finish never consider that X, Y and Z might speak with each other and exchange useful information in the line of duty. If you learn in the end that X "knows," be outraged.

Evaluate them individually, grade each on a scale of one to ten. Select one of them, he who got the highest mark. Decide that he or she is the only one who understood anything whatsoever and act as if the others don't exist. Make up your very own ashram inside of which there are, first and foremost, you and the master, eventually X as well, but certainly not Y or Z, those irritating parasites.

Finally, if you've known the master and the ashram for a relatively long time, play on that shamelessly. It's a trump card you can exploit to counterbalance possible past efforts and compromise any chance for further progress along the way.

Adopt the attitude of the "senior." Come to the ashram as if it were conquered territory. Everyone should immediately sense that the place has no secrets for you, that you know a thing or two about it and didn't arrive yesterday. Brandish a falsely benevolent smile, affect humility. Proceed by allusions, subtly turn conversations so that as quickly as possible they put you in the limelight without your seeming to take part in them. For example, engage a conversation with a relative newcomer and ask him or her, with an air of interest, how long he or she's been coming to the ashram. In turn, he or she'll undoubtedly ask you the same question which will give you the opportunity to answer in detached, factual tones: "Oh, ten (or twenty or thirty) years … " From that point on, don't be stingy with the anecdotes about the "beginnings," "when there were so few of us that the master really made himself available, that one could really 'work in depth' … " Your interlocutor will be fascinated and you get to gloat. As a general rule, treat newcomers or the most recent pupils with superior solicitude. Don't miss an opportunity to counsel, to guide, to accompany, let's just say it, to teach in secret. Hold court, coddle your courtesans. Demonstrate clearly that the members of the master's entourage are your close buddies. Be friends with each one in order to make them powerless, unable to do anything for you. If other members of the old guard are present, adopt with them the attitude of war veterans. Together, endlessly replay the film of the path already taken in order to avoid progressing further along it today. Reminisce about past retreats like real veterans reminisce about past battles. As regards the master's assistants, also "seniors" you undoubtedly knew in their beginnings along the way, be falsely amicable. Claim to aid them in their task of transmission. Intervene to complete or clarify their words. When the occasion presents itself, surreptitiously put them on the spot, always in public of course. Don't doubt for an instant that you could and should be in their place. Above all never conceive that, in the heart of the ashram, the role of a "senior" in the Way – real seniority, moreover, doesn't always measure itself by historic or chronological givens – is to demonstrate (before even opening one's mouth) what the practice can be, and to elevate the atmosphere by his mere presence.

In conclusion, should all these suggestions fail, the Spiritual Enemy offers you, in his infinite unkindness, three glorious possibilities to destroy your chances with both the master and the ashram.

★ "Familiarity breeds contempt," says the proverb. And it's true that we end up ignoring or taking for granted what and who surround us. Drawing inspiration from this truism, make your home in the general vicinity of the ashram. Now that you live "next door," come to the ashram less and less. No longer make retreats, content yourself with "popping in" from time to time to "say hi," attend teaching sessions in a piecemeal fashion, chat with this one or that one. Be a regular without being a pupil anymore.

★ If the ashram hires people for various positions (clerical, etc.), you'll also benefit from trying to become an "employee" of the ashram. This is one of the Spiritual Enemy's greatest strengths: to turn what in itself constitutes a privilege and a rare opportunity into a neutralizer of your sadhana. Take care to make what was a passion into a routine; a vocation into a job; a calling into a sinecure; a risk into a sure thing; a challenge into a constraint. Give precedence to the "functionary" spirit. Put in your hours, refuse to do more, gripe about the benefits, resist any innovation, think about your vacation. Promote inter-personnel conflicts, abuse the little power your position confers on you. Forget completely that you are there to do the best job you can and just hope – but beware, nothing is less sure – that the master is looking the other way.

★ Last and most magnificent strategy: catch *teachitis*. Teachitis is a well-known virus that attacks a large percentage of apprentices of the Way whether they've just arrived or have been there for a while. The people most at risk from the virus are those who offer a socio-professional and/or weak affective breeding ground and consequently have the most accounts to settle.

The telling symptom of contamination is an irrepressible propensity to teach, to transmit, before having been a disciple. The subject can't stop himself from offering lessons, regardless of the fact the master hasn't asked him to do so. In the most benign and short-term cases, teachitis presents itself by the senior's syndrome described above. In the more serious cases the subject sets himself up as a therapist, without any real qualifications, whose intention is to help the others more clearly see that to which he himself is blind. Your affective life is in ruins, your professional life at a standstill, your spiritual life a compensation and an avoidance? Become a therapist. Note that thus establishing oneself as a therapist without even knowing how you really function is the surest way to avoid purging one's unconscious.

In the most serious and almost incurable form of the malady, the subject takes things a step further and, no longer content with his status of therapist-vaguely-teacher, declares himself "awakened" and opens his own "school," thanking the master for his good and loyal services, careful not to offer him the opportunity to respond. At this critical stage, the patient undergoes an irreversible process with more or less dramatic consequences. It should be observed that, at least for a time, the subject always attracts a few pupils, people of good faith not recognizing the symptoms of teachitis and convinced they're dealing with a healthy transmitter.

The Spiritual Enemy has a large number of recruits affected by this malady which, in its most serious form, proves fatal to the way. Of course, if you have the courage to contract the virus in order to definitively destroy your progress along the way, avoid the only known antidote: the pursuit, or the renewal, of a real and sustained relationship with the master.

Ultimate refinement: let's imagine that, despite all the obstacles, you have, *oh horrors*, progressed and proven yourself in the Way sufficiently enough so that the master himself asks you to participate, according to your capacities, in the transmission of the teachings ... This apparently catastrophic situation can turn out to provide you with a new start in your efforts to sabotage your sadhana. The formula is simple: identify yourself with this new role, turn it into a personal success, a diploma of wisdom. Caught up in your functions as an instructor, forget that you are, above all and always, a disciple. The master is your axis, your bearings, your compass, your rampart; therefore keep your distance. Teach more and more, practice less and less, and thus commit spiritual suicide.

Armed with this arsenal of advice, it would take the intervention of God himself to prevent you from succeeding in neutralizing the terrifying danger that the Spiritual Friend presents. Beware of the guru, down with sacred cows.

God? Why not? A master? If one must. Disciple, not on your life.

2

Dozing and Daydreaming

Being Absent from Oneself,
or How Not to Be Vigilant

Be restless and ignore the
Fact that I am God
– *The Bible According to the Spiritual Enemy*

He lived far from himself…
Always inattentive, never
Watchful of himself, keeping
Himself constantly in the absence
Of his creator, he didn't let his
Soul's regard turn inward.
– *Saint Sorcery's Dialogues on
Saint Simpleton*

You've chosen the day and picked
the hour. Therefore, everything
is under control, sleep in peace.
And if ever the Son of man
arrives, he will be an honored
guest, long awaited and received
with great pomp.
– *The Gospel According to the Mind*

Self remembering, presence to one self and to God, keeping the memory of God, awareness … All the spiritual traditions have underscored the fundamental character of conscious attention –

the primary importance of the act of being watchful, called "vigilance" on the Way – whose goal is currently designated by the term "awakening."

Being awakened supposes that one is not sleeping. In order to be sure to continue dozing, like those disciples in the garden despite Christ's exhortation to "keep watch and pray," *underrate vigilance, consider it a practice like any other and not as the condition* sine qua non *of all practice.*

A bad beginning being a giant step towards failure, he or she determined to founder on the way should definitely "get off to a bad start"; otherwise put, "not begin with the beginning." Since vigilance is the basis of the Way and its guiding principle, insist on practicing without it. Put the cart before the horse: forget that practice requires a practitioner and try everything, except vigilance.

Be Dazed and Stay That Way

Firstly, don't be there. Act as if you could follow a Way without first of all working at being the conscious subject of your existence. "Man has no soul," said Mr. Gurdjieff, "but he can create one for himself." Above all do not take the trouble to create a "soul," that stable, interior reference point. Cultivate arrogance and never take things in their proper order. Swelled with non-dualist rhetoric, *imagine you've disappeared as far as ego is concerned, without first having appeared as a person; imagine yourself "dead to this world" without ever having really lived, which is to say having been present in this world.* Fantasize that you're situated in the great beyond of the "subject/object duality" without having so much as arrived at the status of a stable and coherent subject. Decide that you can go directly from the unformed to the formless by short-circuiting the long road of training.

Not being there, you'll be no place at all since the only place you can be is precisely here. Being nowhere, you'll be no one. Not in the ultimate sense (the "there's no one" of the sages who discovered the inexistence of a separate me), but in the most tragically common manner. Being nothing but an individual, you won't reach the status of a true person. Following the example of billions of human beings, you'll be nothing, all things considered, but a complicated animal, a machine that ignores it's a machine.

What, from start to finish of your existence, you will designate by "me," seeing there a coherent and indivisible entity, will be, in reality, a mass of contradictory facets, an amorphous crowd composed of diverse and often antagonistic personae, which won't be aware of one another most of the time anyway. Thus positioned nowhere, scattered by the whim of the winds of your thoughts, desires, fears and identifications, you will be a "nonentity" (Swami Prajnanpad) or, according to Mr. Gurdjieff's more colorful expression, a "shit-ity" – "merdité" in Mr Gurdjieff's peculiar French – sleeping a deep sleep lulled by dreams of awakening.

Consequently, expound upon the "Awakening" as much as you want. Seriously ask yourself whether this one or that one is or is not "awakened," and if you yourself could be awakened one day, with one condition: *never ask yourself to what point you're wakeful here and now.*

In brief, be the least conscious you can be. Think vigilance, discuss vigilance, dream vigilance, but don't keep vigil. Read Krishnamurti without noting that you unthinkingly scratch your nose; burst into the interview room of the Lama with whom you are going to talk consciousness of self without having thought to put your chair back in place and turn off the light in the room you've left; ask the most abstract questions possible; quench yourself with great gulps of interrogation about the nature of pure consciousness while forgetting to be quite simply conscious of yourself – your thoughts, sensations and reactions – at the very moment you ask the questions.

Merely observing that primary instruction – *keep no vigil* – is a guarantee of failure in the Way.

Our entire society being a vast enterprise of organized sleep, you'll have no trouble maintaining your besotted tendencies. It's not a few so-called spiritual readings that are going to shake up the state of unconsciousness that you find normal and even consider, given your spiritual-intellectual interests, as rather enlightened. At most, they will make your dreams sweeter.

If, Devil forbid, you have the bad luck to come into contact with a living teaching, to go to an ashram, monastery or place of retreat, and thus find yourself in an atmosphere more propitious to vigilance, it would be wise to nip any possibility of gaining experience in the bud.

Continuous Control

First golden rule: *avoid simplicity*. Cultivate the abstract, the over-complicated, the inextricable. Remember that *that which is badly conceived is confusedly pronounced* and that obscure directives will result in an unclear practice. Also, you'll need to fabricate the most complicated conception of vigilance possible for yourself.

Begin by seeing vigilance as an almost superhuman effort leading to an absolute control. Does the ego, your ego, dream of being all-powerful, does it want to be the supreme Kontroler of a universe at its mercy? Very well. Vigilance must only be approached from this perspective – that of the master of the world. Let the ego imagine a vigilance for the ego, by the ego and of the ego that serves its lust for domination.

Along the same lines *confuse vigilance with concentration*. Turn this into a matter of will, an irritating attitude that results in a total absence of the natural. Think of vigilance as close surveillance of the ego on itself twenty-four hours a day. Construct yourself a vigilance – a prison wall behind which you'll be both the prisoner and the guard standing in his watchtower, gun in hand ready to stop the slightest unpredicted action against the rules.

This conception of vigilance will allow you to progress stiffly through existence, the brow furrowed, eyebrows lowered, jaw clenched, arms and legs rigid, eyes fixed.

Other than the fact that you will find no pleasure in living, you'll quickly arrive at either a negative accounting favorable to discouragement and self-disparagement or, in case of "success," to a state of saturation that will provoke an opposite reaction leading you to total dispersion.

In brief, make vigilance a continuous control before you ever get out of the starting block, which is to say, the simple consciousness of being.

I Am That Which I Am Not

That simple consciousness of being, flee it, avoid it at all costs. To become familiar with it will risk greatly compromising your chances of failure on the Way.

Pretending to seek vigilance, open your eyes wide, look

right and left, up, down and sideways, but never in the middle of your own center. Never, in any case, take the trouble to consider the obvious: here and now, I am. I exist and I know it. I know it because I feel it. Content yourself with eventually knowing it: make this into an intellectual conviction nourished by vedantic readings that allow you to pontificate, to proceed by a comparative approach of the concept "I am" one finds in Nisargadatta Maharaj, Ramana Maharshi, and the Old Testament ("I am who I am"). This cultural diversion will present no danger, provided that your knowledge never becomes comprehension. Know that you are but don't feel it. Stay trapped at the level of the head without plunging into the sensual experience of the consciousness of being. Let your reference be either "mystical transport," "ecstasy," the "magic moment" or the "supra-conscience." Thus occupied with searching for a particular state that can turn you into someone special, you'll bypass the normal state in which you would have found yourself banally happy. Desperately chase after an experience that's extraordinary and rarely attained in order not to seek repose in an experience that's ordinary and always available to the consciousness of being, the source and domain of all experience. Pursue the incredible to better avoid the obvious: you are.

Briefly stated, *Let it never occur to you to ask yourself if you are here and now*. The mere fact of turning your attention in this direction would lead you to ascertain that, in reality, you are, which would naturally further lead you to letting down your guard. Therefore, force yourself to exercise constant control of your physical, emotional and mental manifestations without directing your vision toward the source of all these manifestations – that is to say, *consciousness*, an origin that is also the natural regulator. Like the perfect grind at the school of the awakening, insist on regulating your functioning by yourself rather than returning inward to life itself. Be an ego scrutinizing itself in the mirror; do not relax in the consciousness of being. The intelligence of life would then take over your own intelligence and the self-dictatorship would be shaken.

See in vigilance a supra-conscience, a summit scaled by sheer will rather than a simple return to the self, to you yourself in your own intrinsic dignity. Be careful never to find this "you, yourself," to your liking. If by chance a serene moment favorable to the presentiment of the profoundness presents itself at a bend of your existence, don't profit from it. Right away, find something to do, preoccupations to ruminate, no matter what, provided you do not seize the opportunity to know that you are. "Be anxious and know not that I am God." Having no other reference than that of getting carried away by ordinary fits of anger and dispersion, you can only turn vigilance into an obscure and constricted concept.

If, having unfortunately come into contact with a living teaching, you see yourself offered, *oh horrors*, the practice of certain exercises, which supposedly favor the presence of the self, it would behoove you to mock, without a moment's hesitation, the fundamental principles.

Every spiritual tradition having placed the memory or the recall of self at the heart of its practical mechanism, a wide variety of exercises exists aimed at facilitating the experience, from sitting meditation to diverse forms of dynamic meditation, rituals, prayers, tea ceremonies, martial arts, calligraphy, archery and other disciplines whose reason for being resides not so much in the results obtained as in the opportunity provided through them to become one with oneself.

All these exercises are based on a single principle that it's important to identify so that you will be able to pervert it.

If Your Eye Is Unsound, Your Entire Body Is in Obscurity

The state of self-remembering suddenly appears when you function simultaneously on the physical, emotional and mental levels; consciousness being the unifying element. Each time you are simultaneously conscious of your present reality on the three levels – in your body, heart and mind – a light deep within you illuminates, that "eye" opens, the eye Christ asserted was "the body's lamp," adding: "If your eye is sound (i.e., unified) your entire body is in the light." It's therefore important that your eye not be "sound " but sick, complex, multiple, so that you remain plunged in obscurity, " … there where exist tears and the gnashing of teeth."

Vigilance is based on the principle of unification. It's a matter of passing from a scattered, piecemeal condition to a unified, assembled condition. *The secret of non-vigilance – and therefore of non-practice since vigilance is the condition* sine qua non *of practice – consists in mocking, every instant, this princi-ple of unification and substituting the principle of division in its place*. The guarantee for non-presence and forgetfulness of self will be to make an effort to act divided – head, body and heart deaf and blind one unto the other, functioning disjointedly like an orchestra without a conductor in which each musician obsti-nately plays his part at his own rhythm and whim, never wor-rying about the harmony of the ensemble.

To get off to a good start in the application of the princi-ple of division, *avoid all conscious relation to the body*. The lat-ter can reveal itself, as will later be explained in detail, to be a dangerous support for vigilance, so it's important to immediate-ly neutralize the help it can provide. Restrict yourself to a mechanical use of this miraculous instrument.

Not the Body One Is but the Body One Has

As regards this point, the key formula is the following: not *the body one is* but *the body one has* – that is, the body con-sidered as an extension and a consumable good of me, the owner, the ego's docile valet, the owner having all the rights.

In regard to a slave, two attitudes are possible: a negli-gence bordering on the scornful or even abusive – the body is a work horse that I use for my own ends, exploiting it to the max-imum while giving it the minimum of care; or a fanatical atten-tion aimed toward ever increasing performance. In both cases, the body is not a respected servant of the being, but an object devoted to me, either mistreated or idolized.

On this point, as on so many others, our society will be your greatest ally. The cult of one's own body instantly obliter-ates any approach to the body that *one is*.

In its marvelous perversity, our culture encourages all the outrages against the body – total lack of physical exercise; unbalanced and excessive food habits, tobacco, alcohol, drugs, over-consumption of medicines with uncontested side-effects; polluted air; an infernal pace; constant pressure; diverse and varied excesses – while at the same time, on all fronts, it exalts the image of the ideal body: young, beautiful according to cur-rent standards, efficient, sexually desirable. The system is so well oiled that no matter which attitude you adopt, it would be difficult not to be subjugated by the unrestricted reign of the *body one has*.

In this context so favorable to non-practice, choose the attitude best suited to your penchants.

If laziness and inertia are congenital factors, *avoid on principle all physical activity*. By favoring energetic circulation and, thus, corporal alertness, regular exercise could unfittingly lead to a natural vigilance. Therefore don't hesitate to let yourself go downhill as far as taking care of your body is concerned. Find a way to ensure that the body you were given as a vehicle for inner maturation deteriorates as quickly as possible like a house or car given no maintenance. Keep it stiff, tensed, heavy, encumbered with toxins. Remember that a slovenly body can only contribute to the degradation you intend to cultivate.

If, on the other hand, your temperament and habits incline you toward physical activity, never fear: nothing's easier than perverting that which, in itself, constitutes a more or less healthy propensity. Only pay attention to your body with the aim of turning it into the display window of your vanity, a superb screen capable of hiding the repressed misery in the back shop. Don't content yourself with treating your body with the respect and care due a faithful servant; treat it with the obsessive spirit of those who, completely identified with their property, tend their house, garden and car with maniacal attention.

Do as you please provided that *physical exercise plays no part in deepening the sentiment of being, but reinforces your dominant spirit of having*. Do not seek to be more aware of the flow of life, in and of itself, by relying on an alert body; just be intent on having good musculature, a sculptural anatomy, a dazzling physical aspect ...

Thus practiced, sport will prove itself, in more ways than one, to be marvelously harmful to your spiritual maturation. Other than the fact that your ego will swell at the same time as your biceps and that your pride will follow the rising curve of your performance, physical activity, thus cultivated, will constitute an efficient buffer against latent emotions. Here again, your Spiritual Enemy encourages you to corrupt a practice, *a priori* beneficial, by intervening in the dosage. It only takes a little excess to turn physical maintenance and a healthy evacuation of surface tension through well-tempered exercise into a systematic avoidance of feeling; sport thus becoming the best ally of repression.

In fact, and your Enemy can't help but rejoice in this, a number of experienced athletes begin and then continue a sport as an unconscious survival strategy in order not to succumb to tensions apt to destroy them. Over time, this instrument of their structure and fulcrum of their survival becomes the most solid obstacle to the advent of a vulnerability indispensable to inner opening.

In physical performance, valued by a society dedicated to "winners," they find the justification for flight in the face of underlying fears and tensions. Through one of those magic tricks, your Enemy (who incessantly tries to make you believe the moon is made of green cheese) just *loves* what is (in fact) avoidance, but which appears to the world's eyes to be a demonstration of courage.

Also, it would be a shame, if you're naturally inclined towards sports, not to use them as an anaesthetic when all and sundry encourage you to do just that. Therefore, become addicted to those endorphins secreted each time you move. Jogging every morning, intensive bodybuilding, drastic gymnastics, etc., let your ego dictate an implacable pace. Remember that *in every domain excess guarantees bad positioning*. Feel ill at ease as soon as you haven't biked five miles, run for an hour or swum five hundred laps. Keep giving yourself new challenges. Use an afternoon off to hop around, sweat, exhaust yourself. *Avoid rest, it might reveal latent anxieties and other subterranean problems*. Along this line, become an adept of exploit leisure activities, performance vacations, and long-distance-race days off. Stun your body, wear out your heart, stupefy yourself through physical activity. That way, you will be both cut off from and content with yourself.

If, nevertheless, you're not attracted by the traditional athletic disciplines but lean more towards yoga, tai-chi, qi-gong, and other practices with a spiritual connotation, there again, nothing is lost. True, with the right transmission and practices these exercises can prove dangerous for your failure in the Way. They may promote, over and above better health, a refinement of sentiments, energetic circulation, a taking-root, and therefore vigilance. However, those corporal approaches lend themselves, as much if not more than the others, to corruption.

Begin by applying the always profitable principle of superiority.

Regard yourself as being above the currently unrefined approach to sports. In the manner of certain adherents of natural cures – wilfully condescending of "official" medicine and its practitioners; those conspirators in a system deemed worthy of the mafia; poor slobs conditioned by ten years of university studies, internship and other bastions of a retrograde mentality – look down on the ordinary run of athletes who "only" work their bodies, pursuing performance … ignorant, poor things, of chakras, meridians, and other fine energy sources. What's more, as subtle as they may be, these approaches can entirely nourish the most unrefined of pretensions. Nothing prevents you from flaunting your superb yoga postures as others flaunt their muscles in front of the mirror, or from showing yourself off in your neighborhood park by giving, as if it were nothing, admirable demonstrations of tai-chi-chuan.

Once the principle of superiority is well in place, the surest method of making bodywork serve "having" rather than "being" will be *to insist that it, in and of itself, constitutes a path to liberation*. Whether you practice yoga, tai-chi, or even a martial art, attribute possibilities that it doesn't have (or no longer has) to your discipline of choice. In the name of a past that is certainly real, but belonging to an entirely different culture and radically different context (in which yoga, tai-chi or the martial arts were studied with a spiritual master, and part of an integral path), act as if the exercise in itself, preferably accompanied by a dusting of theory and spiritualizing considerations, constitutes "a path" in the fullest sense of the term. See the tree as the forest and, due to the simple fact that you give yourself over to, let's say, yoga, a little seriously and assiduously, consider yourself "committed to a path." You'll have no trouble finding encouragement in this direction. An abuse of language has quickly developed and the common horde is rife with teachers who, although they don't always admit it, feed as much on the positive projections and fantasies of their students as on their financial participation. Therefore, don't content yourself with one of those honest yoga professors who is, perhaps, open to the dimension the positions issue from, but who doesn't insist on doing more than help to sound them out; join, preferably, the small, select courtesans of your neighborhood yogi-therapist-guru.

Briefly, in the manner of those "traditional" athletes, use

yoga or any other similar discipline as an *avoidance strategy*.

Spiritualizing Materialism

Finally, and this last perversity is particularly tasty, use work on the body and its little extras to cultivate, in the name of spirituality and without ever realizing it, the most unbridled materialism.

It's one of your Enemy's deepest motives for rejoicing to verify that the champions of the New Age, like a lot of seekers a tad more serious, have, in all unconsciousness, made the founding postulate of materialism their own – that's to say, that the body and matter create and determine the spirit, and not the reverse. Ah, if they only knew how much pleasure the Prince of the Earth takes in watching them reduce spiritual awakening to a subtle chemistry susceptible of being manipulated provided one has the required knowledge as concerns "chakras," "energies," and other meridians ... How he appreciates that new, disguised scientism, which only differs from its past version in that it depends on the vague rather than on the rigorous. Whatever the difference, it is but so similar in its control obsession, its will to dominate life by mastering the mechanism ... How he savors the emergence of a spiritualizing ideology behind which hides the grimacing mask of materialism.

Take a truth, for example that of the interconnection between the somatic and psychological realms, then distort it to the advantage of the Kontroler ego: systematically make reference to it, reducing it to a handful of simplistic affirmations (if you have cancer it's because ... , that disease means ... "). You can thus make those who are sick feel guilty; you can even feel guilty yourself if, *oh unthinkable eventuality*, your own health gives you cause for concern. Given that possibility – to fall quite simply ill – act as if you can't even conceive of it. *Cultivate the fantasy of perfect health* with the added help of special diets and medical practices where treatment tends to be a philosophical discourse. From the lofty heights of the "work" you're considering "doing on yourself," never envisage that you, like the rest of the world, can finally succumb to cancer, a heart attack or even be inflicted by a run-of-the-mill allergy.

To sum things up, do everything possible in order, in one form or another, to be and remain badly positioned in relation to the body, the essential thing being to reinforce the identification (*the body one has*) rather than to diminish its hold by approaching more closely *the body one is*.

Don't Be Where The Body Is

Nevertheless, the body has more than one trick up its sleeve. After all, isn't it animated by the infinite intelligence of life? Simple attention to *the body one is* can seriously imperil the division that's indispensable to non-vigilance.

Never forget that all consciousness of the body threatens your non-practice. The body is, in effect, dangerous in that it doesn't know how to be anywhere but here and at any other moment than now. As long as I live, I have a body at my disposal, which, unable to find itself nowhere, is always somewhere. This somewhere where the body finds itself is always *here*. And, this moment the body finds itself in is always *now*. A terrifying menace, therefore, this never-absent body, always present and invariably here and now.

You know very well that the key to non-practice consists in not being present here and now but, on the contrary, absent, elsewhere, lost in the meanderings of the past and future. Therefore, beware of the body, that perpetually available fulcrum already situated here and now … It's no surprise that all the spiritual teachings make such a fuss about it!

If there's one question you should avoid asking yourself, it's certainly the following: Am I there where the body is? *Make it a rule not to be where the body is. Do not be what you appear to be.*

This directive, however essential, is no less simple to apply under all circumstances.

When, for example, you descend the stairs, interiorly be everything but a human being descending the stairs. *Let there be no accord between appearance and being.* Therefore, although you appear to descend the staircase step by step, be, in fact, a son-in-law busy settling his accounts with his mother-in-law; a wife enumerating her husband's faults; or, if your preferences run to less mundane realistic scenarios, a star accepting the applause of a crowd of fans; a guru awash in the veneration of his adoring flock, etc. In fact, your range of choices is as wide as your imagination, since your mind can present you with every conceivable elsewhere. In practice, little does it matter which film the mind programs provided there is no relation between what you are doing and what you are.

In order not to be what you appear to be, to assure you're not where the body is, *avoid seeking support from the present posture*.

Never worry about the manner in which you're physically there. Just as it doesn't know how to be nowhere, but is always somewhere (that's to say *here*), at every moment the body is in one position or another.

The body without a posture doesn't exist. *The body one has* takes its posture automatically, according to a collection of habits, most of them bad; *the body one is* consciously positions itself to serve the intentions of he or she who keeps watch. All consciousness of the present posture is consequently to be proscribed, since it constitutes a step in the direction of *the body one is*. Thus, you must resolutely remain unconscious of the position you're in at any given instant.

Above all, do not take this recommendation lightly: to convince you of the danger, note, in the different traditions, the prestige allotted to the adoption of a posture, whether that means the Zen monk seated in meditation, the Moslem accomplishing his prayers on a rug, the crouching Egyptian scribe, the yogi in lotus position, the Christian on his knees with hands joined, etc. Note that the saints, sages, kings and other figures supposed to impose respect are always represented in a dignified position. Whatever the latter is – standing, seated, or even prone in the manner of certain Buddhas reclining with the head resting on a hand – it confers them a certain bearing. *Thus it is important that you have no bearing*. Do not accord so much as a hint of interest to the manner in which you hold yourself, that's to say, to the manner in which you inhabit your body.

On this point as on so many others, our society will be your greatest ally. Its cult worship directed at *the body one has* – the body one would like to have and keep, one that pays off sexually, which is to say is considered lovable – instantly obliterates any approach to the body one is. What with the couches you sink into, seats that bend your body, the easy chairs that swallow you, the schools where you learn to live with shoulders raised, back bent and hand tightly gripping a pen so that later you can continue on to an office, fingers curved into claws over the keyboard ... society perpetuates a world where no one knows any longer how to position their body. It has substituted gestures with gesticulations; posture with contortions; presence with attitudes; etc. Constrained from childhood in your natural propensity to sit with legs crossed, trained to throw out your chest and suck in your stomach, surrounded by the limp or the rigid from the start, you won't have the merest notion of a correct posture, that's to say, one that conforms with the laws of nature. Better yet, any invitation to work even a little on the way you are physically there, to seek a rooted verticality, will so thoroughly begin to produce an echo in you of old injunctions ("Stand straight"!) that, in order to continue, you'll need to overcome a psychological resistance as well as the inevitable bodily aches and pains engendered by your attempts to put things back in order.

With a little luck, you'll go no further, and grow old in a body you don't inhabit. Whether you accord it fanatical care in order to conserve, as long as possible, its book value as a desirable body, or you allow it to go to ruin, joining the horde of neglected bodies, it will resemble an empty shell and remain deserted, there, where there's not a sign of life.

Suck In Your Stomach, Throw Out Your Chest

At this point your Spiritual Enemy must warn you against two dangerous factors which might prove helpful to self remembering and therefore must be short-circuited at all costs: breathing and placing your attention in the lower abdomen.

Beware of breathing. Witness of the movement of life within us, breathing could, if you have the unfortunate idea of paying attention to it, constitute a direct link to body consciousness and thus be an access to here and now. Breathing manifests itself only in the instant. Therefore, it is necessary to avoid all recourse to that help, as evident as it is subtle. *Do not breathe consciously; never even consider, when you feel yourself being carried away by the current of existence, to return to yourself via attention to breath.* Never think to simply inhale and exhale consciously on a daily basis, especially when an emotion threatens to precipitate you out of yourself.

Thus avoiding all conscious breathing, don't allow yourself to direct the breath toward the lower abdomen. Take care to remain like the better part of your contemporaries deprived of a real center of gravity. Faithful to the prejudices of a society that worships the flat belly and is condescending – yet, at the same time, complacent – toward what is located "below the belt," never glimpse the importance of what Japanese tradition calls the "*hara*" – reintroduced in the West by that harmful Graf Dürckheim – and which one finds in Christian statuary under the name of the "Gothic stomach." *Empty-bellied, everything in the head, emotions slung across the back, be the one who is always "out of sorts."* This neglect of breathing accompanied by an ignorance of the hara should assure you of remaining deprived of a base; lacking stability; carried away by the agitation born of and fueled by thoughts, so you can go on your way, stomach in and shoulders raised, a straw swirling in the winds of existence.

Meditate to Escape

If, nevertheless, to the great pleasure of your faithful Enemy, you stubbornly frequent ashrams, monasteries, spiritual centers and other places offering salvation, but which often prove to be places of perdition, you won't be able to avoid encountering meditation, the universal exercise proposed in all the existing paths. Potentially dangerous for your non-practice, this discipline can easily be gotten around. It only takes a little bad faith applied with persistence. Here are a few suggestions.

Remembering the importance of poor posture, *begin by pretending to meditate without seriously worrying about positions.* Used to holding your body any which way, do not seize the opportunity of an initiation to meditation in order to change your habits. Have the incoherence to approach the exercise often called "sitting" without taking the trouble to learn how to sit. Decide right away that the proposed posture, generally with the buttocks on a cushion, crossed legs touching the floor, is "too hard for you." Feebly attempt it once, just to say you have tried for appearance's sake, then give up at the first twinge of pain. Justify your inability to be asked to make the slightest effort with an argument that stresses the necessity to not abuse oneself, and the absurdity of useless suffering. *Confuse goodwill with complacency, exigency with mistreatment.* Never take into consideration, even for an instant, the fact that generations of meditators have, for millenniums, taken the trouble to accustom themselves to a traditional posture in order to later reap its benefits. In brief, don't give yourself the slightest chance to find yourself one day at ease in a posture which in itself is a teaching. In order not to isolate yourself from the flock, sit, but in any which way. Let your posture be a caricature. Shamelessly scoff at the laws of correct positioning, beginning with the law of taking root. At most, set the buttocks down on the cushion, but do not set yourself down. Take care to keep your knees in the air. If you pretend to meditate seated on a chair, do not place your feet firmly on the ground. The important thing is to not provide yourself with a base so as to assure that a little push will suffice to destabilize you. The principle of stability thus evacuated, you'll naturally make a mockery of that of verticality, because it depends on taking root. Knees in the air, curve the back, which will guarantee that you feel nothing in the spinal column other than a familiar oppression accentuated by the constraint of that exercise. To perfect the masquerade, stretch the neck, forward or backward as you wish, provided that, the back of the neck not being in the extension of the spinal column, the head is not aligned. Finally, lightly trample the principle of immobility. Don't envision the possibility of staying still more than a few seconds. At the first itch or tingle, the merest discomfort, the least little sign of a cramp, or quite simply as soon as you begin to feel bored, move. You'll discover that, as far as physical immobility is concerned during meditative practice, the law of "all or nothing" applies: to assure transforming meditation into St. Vitus's dance, you need only set the pace by moving around on the slightest pretext. Consequently, from the very beginning look for a more comfortable position for the legs, scratch that itchy nose, take out a handkerchief and clear your blocked sinuses – it being understood that, to save appearances, these gesticulations need be accomplished with great solemnity: don't just scratch, lift the arm slowly and scratch your nostrils with an air of penetration before religiously resting your hand back on your knee; don't whip out your handkerchief, extract it laboriously while keeping the eyes half-closed, then blow your nose with unction … the operation needing of course, to be repeated at regular intervals during the entire time imparted to meditation in order to guarantee the impossibility of a semblance of inner recollection. You will thus deprive yourself of an occasion to train yourself in non-identification with regard to physical sensation as well as psychological fluctuations. *Fidget, be identified, capitulate in the face of the slightest mechanical impulse.* Above all, don't take the time to watch the appearance of that impulse, to look at it a little while and then realize that having reached its peak, it goes the same way it came. Such an observation stemming from the supporting point of the respected posture would teach you more about non-identification and the insubstantiality of the phenomena than volumes of philosophy. Once again, stuff yourself with non-dualist readings, hold forth on the subject of forms taken by the formless and other fads that appear and disappear at the surface of consciousness, as long as you never give yourself the opportunity to experience it in a simple and concrete manner.

What if pride prevents you from not cutting a good figure during meditation? In case you prefer to revert to the more flattering panoply of the impeccable meditator rather than ostentatiously fidgeting, don't despair: thanks to the Kontroler's strategy, you can make a mockery of the laws of practice while still saving appearances.

The recipe is simple, it only takes applying the above mentioned principle of dictatorial vigilance to meditation. *Confuse intention with will, attention and concentration*; do not distinguish control – a limit tranquilly set on the pretended almighty power of mechanicalness – from Kontrol, that merciless refusal and repression of mechanisms. Establish a police state calling, sooner or later, for a reaction-revolution. Put all your money not on letting go, but on a steel fist in a concrete glove. Tense yourself in order not to flinch, restrain the slightest motion, ruthlessly put down every attempt at rebellion on the physical, emotional and mental levels. With all bad will as regards your functioning, repress your thoughts, nip agitation in the bud, put a lid on the fomenting of your emotions. If an impulse to move appears, refuse it, feel only anger and scorn toward that mechanism which just should not exist.

Briefly stated, *do not meditate with, meditate against.* Turn meditation into an exhausting battle, a division rather than a unification, a fight to the death between your great disciple's ego and the actual reality of your mechanisms. You will thus be sure not to experience that letting go which is the result of acceptance associated with benevolent control. The meditation session over, you'll leave either the winner – head high, proud not to have batted an eyelash, straight as a stick and wound up as tightly as a spring; or you'll leave the vanquished – disgusted and discouraged, exuding self-scorn, furious at not having been the strongest.

The worst needing always to be considered, let's imagine that you stubbornly insist on meditating correctly: nothing is lost. The so-called awakening exercises, even correctly practiced, can always be perverted in such a manner that they actually maintain sleep.

The fact of starting, or ending, your day by meditating presents no risk to your pursuit of spiritual coma provided that this meditative parenthesis remains precisely a parenthesis with no relation to the instant-by-instant of daily life. In fact, the connoisseurs of deviltry will opt for this refinement, which constitutes an exercise assiduously practiced according to the rules, without that having the slightest effect as concerns personal growth.

The recipe for a meditation in and of itself correctly practiced, but nevertheless perfectly sterile, is elementary: *decide that the practice of the path is summed up by the exercise of sitting meditation.* Seeing as you're not a monk residing in a Zen monastery and thus consecrating the greater part of your days to zazen or to sitting in silence, this simple positioning will guarantee that the time dedicated each day to effective practice of the Way shrinks ineluctably. In order not to progress on the path, as with any artistic, athletic or creative discipline, you need only to practice not enough or not at all. One can, let's repeat this, think about it and discuss it to the heart's content. It is even recommended to confuse ideas, conversations and readings on practice with the practice itself; to fabricate an imaginary practice as a substitute for real practice, the essential thing being always and forever, whatever you say and think, to not practice.

The assimilation of sitting meditation to practice will assure you thirty minutes, an hour at most, of daily practice versus thirteen or fourteen hours of intense non-practice. *Do not envision meditation as a preparation or a dress rehearsal for practice, but as the practice itself.* Let meditation be for you what the weekly religious service is for the so-well-called "Sunday Christians": a convenient observance in that it gives the sentiment of duty-done, and dispenses one from later putting into practice the precepts in whose name it was created. In the manner of so many of the faithful who, in all good conscience, make a mockery of the Gospel as soon as they leave the church, take care that no relation is established between meditation and daily life. Consider the sitting position a pose more than a posture. When morning meditation ends, consider practice terminated. Above all, do not envision that it, on the contrary, can begin at that very moment. *Make a big deal of formal meditation to better forget informal meditation.* Attach the greatest importance to the sitting position in order to completely bypass meditation in action – the only meditation capable of allowing you to really progress; the essential thing being that your days are spent, not in sitting meditation, but in action.

Set non-practice going first thing in the morning by getting up in a reactional manner. Leave the dojo, zendo or meditation hall completely carried away. Deem that, after a period of immobility, you've earned the right to move around a bit, march quickly to the exit, distractedly put on your shoes with a series of brisk, mechanical gestures. Hurry off to breakfast, your head infested with diverse and varied thoughts, paying not the slightest attention to the way you move through space. You'll thus permit the eventual benefits of meditation to evaporate in just a few seconds. The moment you sit down to the first meal of the day, you need to be already scattered to the four winds.

Live Mechanically

All that remains to be done now is to let yourself be swept along by the blind dynamic whose plaything you've been since birth.

The important thing is to remain faithful to the principle of division and thus *to pay neither attention nor care to the elementary daily gestures.* Under this heading, meals constitute particularly propitious moments for non-practice, marvelous opportunities for unconsciousness and dispersion. Resolutely begin by mocking the very idea of vigilance right there at break-fast. Sit any which way, all worries about correct posture forgotten as soon as meditation has ended. Serve yourself copiously. From start to finish of the meal, chatter without the slightest notion of what you are actually saying or what you've eaten, although you've shoveled in excessive amounts of food.

Above all, do not try to consciously accomplish the gestures necessary to feed yourself; manipulate knife, fork and spoon with no restraint. As to ingesting the food, don't eat it, gulp it down. It's not a question of savoring what's in your mouth but of filling yourself up as quickly as possible in an attempt, as desperate as it is unconscious, to fill an inner void. This mechanical relationship to food presents many advantages in terms of non-practice: not only are you in a state of total absence, but your very distraction doesn't permit you to actually taste what you're absorbing and, simultaneously, in no way favors moderation. In effect, the less you take pleasure in tasting, the more you need to compensate quality by quantity, the more you weigh yourself down, which consequently induces a physiological state of heaviness hardly propitious to the act of keeping vigil. Furthermore, an excessive absorption of food almost always accompanies a feeling of vague guilt nourishing numerous ideas and emotions that will estrange you even further from yourself. What is gained is, therefore, considerable and multidimensional from the point of view of sabotage. Adopt the rule to always leave the table with stomach full to bursting, with the sensation that you can't swallow another bit without risking to explode. The subtle energy that's indispensable to presence will thus be mobilized to accomplish the laborious process of digestion. In summary: *eat without consciousness, therefore without pleasure, and without moderation.*

If you find yourself on retreat at a monastery or ashram where meals are eaten in silence, take pleasure in perverting this invitation to vigilance. Don't use the absence of words to go within, but on the contrary, make use of that opportunity to think more than ever, to get lost in thoughts, fantasies and favorite scenarios. Let your motto be: *the less I speak, the more I think.*

When the moment to clear the table comes, force yourself to make the greatest possible racket. Grab your plate, noisily slam the silverware on it, then rush to the sink where you'll participate in washing the dishes in the same frantic manner. Make sure the façade of silence maintained at the table is followed by a cacophonous explosion that amply compensates it.

If meals constitute golden opportunities for non-vigilance, this is also true for every moment and every situation. *Every place is a place to not be, to daydream, to fritter about, to lose patience, to be agitated.* Every gesture is an invitation to hurry, to do things haphazardly and to create a mess.

Generally speaking, in order not to be vigilant, find support in the thousands of simple gestures indispensable to daily living. Consider everyday activities – bathing, dressing, etc. – as chores that are inevitable but devoid of interest. Execute motions at lightning speed, expedite the smallest task with just one aim in mind: to be done with it as quickly as possible. Simply functioning from day to day leads you to enter into contact with a great number of objects. Be brutal with these objects. Cultivate disrespect towards these things, which you nevertheless need. Yank open doors then slam them shut, mistreat chairs, throw shoes and clothing around, etc. The simple gesture of opening and closing a door, to pick up or set down an object should never be a reminder, an opportunity to remember yourself. Always accomplish it mechanically, carelessly and without love.

In the same fashion, each day contains multiple moments of transition. Above all, do not entertain the idea of using these moments as so many opportunities to return to yourself, to train yourself in being here and now. When you need to go from one room to another, to stand, to sit, to dress, to undress, to get in or out of your car, to walk, to cross a street, to climb the stairs, pay no attention to what you are doing. See these passages as a waste of time, something to be gotten through with impatience and dispersion. Never take advantage of these moments called "empty" which can, if you don't watch out, prove to be propitious to the approach of fullness. Each time you wait (for a bus, a subway, an elevator, an appointment to arrive, the light to turn green, etc.) turn the moment into a stress festival, a peak of impatience, a rocket burst of denial. Above all, do not let go, don't use the moment to exhale from your abdomen and feel the completeness of the instant. Feel desperate, tensed toward a goal situated in the future (the arrival of the bus, subway, appointment, etc.) and in whose absence, it's understood, you can't possibly feel whole. When you have to wait in line, stamp your foot, fuss, fume. Do not place yourself solidly on both feet in order to feel your presence. Stiffly shuffle, instead, from one foot to the other, practice the dance of the irritated person. In the doctor's or dentist's waiting room, never let it occur to you to sit calmly, back straight and both feet firmly on the floor in order to breathe and contemplate. Hardly taking time to perch yourself on the edge of the seat, open your eyes wide then frantically grab a magazine that you'll thumb through like an automaton. The important thing is to fill time, to never allow yourself the least chance to get in touch with your inner depth.

In thus positioning yourself, you'll be assured to never catch a glimpse of the possibility of waiting without waiting, to take a vacation with every parenthesis daily life offers. All the intervals between two parentheses will remain dead time rather than being converted into living time, reminders and occasions for finding oneself.

Your enemy takes the liberty to insist on this point, for there are, in a day, many short periods thus employed commuting from one point to another, performing routine but indispensable activities. Think of the risk of a greater vigilance, and thus progress on the path you would run if you took into account the potential of those moments ... Consequently, it is crucial that you persist in living them as mechanically as you possibly can.

In short, *dream as much as you want of the "essential," provided you always avoid offering yourself the possibility of coming into contact with it by leaning on the existential* as it exists here and now. The cause is understood: the existential conditions are never those you need in order to be vigilant. Let the essential always be in far-off lands, something for tomorrow, under other conditions. You would willingly practice vigilance if ... if you were a monk, swami in India, on retreat in an ashram, married, divorced, with another woman, another man, on vacation ... anywhere, but certainly not there where you are, busy sorting through the boring mail filled with bills and ads. Ferociously oppose the "relative," the dreary reality, and the "Absolute," that great elsewhere, and assure that the two never meet. In theory, live only for "the vertical dimension," of which you will be a chatty apostle; in practice, vegetate on the surface, confined to the uniquely existential dimension, without according the tiniest amount of space to the essential (other than in your thoughts), in order to maintain the spiritual fantasy that replaces, so advantageously, practice.

Along the lines of the preceding indications, you'll profit from remaining always *strained toward*. Never be exactly there where you are and involved in what you're doing, but always out of sync, several steps in advance of where your feet are. When you accomplish an activity, whatever it is, push toward the results. If, for example, you load the dishwasher, begin by wishing you'd already finished. When you go from one place to another, start off with the desire to already be there. Apply *this principle of "time-lagging forward"* to the merest gesture. Do nothing, including going to the bathroom or washing your hands, without refusing the notion that it's not already done. Besides the fact that continual application of this principle will rob all your gestures of gracefulness and complicate your life by causing you to commit many more errors than if you acted calmly, it will guarantee you uninterrupted non-vigilance.

Egomobile Steering

On this subject your Enemy recommends you spend lots of time in the car, the automobile being a privileged place to train yourself to be strained toward. Perhaps a better expression is "egomobile," seeing as the sacrosanct "jalopy" has, in our society, mutated into a symbolic extension of the self – a closed and protected place where one can nevertheless apprehend the world by what one sees through the window, and be in contact with others while at the same time remaining separate; a tiny bubble, centered around the driver-owner proudly seated at the commands, eventually surrounded by passengers who, while they're incorporated into the driver's small world, find themselves subjected to his will because they don't drive … Yes, the car is a veritable ego on wheels. From his position of control (look at the way all car ads insist on the notion of "power" and "control"), the driver aggressively launches himself into an encounter with an "exterior" world reputed to belong to him, reserved for his personal use and, as such, subject to his personal pleasure.

The egomobilist rolls along "his" road where, at the bend,

he passes a more or less large number of others who, it's understood, drive "badly" – in any case, not as well as he – and, at any rate, have the impudence to block his path or force him to slow down in his implacable pursuit when they shouldn't, in fact, even be there.

Thus, take full advantage of this privileged space that the car provides to cultivate non-vigilance. Identify with your vehicle, that brilliant showcase of your majestic self. As soon as you get in it, drop your inhibitions and other superfluous social conventions. You are the master, God of the asphalt, king of the road, which amounts to saying "of the universe." Your first rule should be to never respect the speed limit. On foot, you have to follow the rules; but once in your car, you are untouchable, subjected to no other law but your own, the only legitimate one. Forge ahead then. The world is yours, and the only right the others have is to respectfully move aside and let you pass. If they have a momentary lapse, put them in their place, that's to say, the side of the road, quickly reminding them of their inferior status with loud honks of the horn that oblige them to comply immediately. Does another dare, the bumpkin, to hesitate a second before pulling to the right or left while, ever proud and sure, you continue resolutely on your way? Deafen him with your horn without giving him another thought, then, as you pass him, inundate him with curses that you would never dare pronounce on the street, but which, enclosed in your carriage, you feel authorized to proffer at the encounter of the poor beggar who, guilty of the crime of *lèse-majesté*, has dared to make you "lose a few seconds," to slow the rhythm of that conquest that even the shortest trip becomes for you. And if the unthinkable arrives, if some bastard has, on this highway – the theatre of your exploits – the audacity to pass you, don't give an inch. Chase after him, pass him in turn at the first opportunity to show him your superiority as well as his own fathomless insignificance. Beware, you wimps, and make room for the master! Stop signs, speed limits, big deal … It's understood that these regulations, certainly necessary for others, don't apply to that very special driver which is you, and that any intervention intended to make you respect them is an outrage.

In sum, *every time you get in the car, make sure it's your ego that gets behind the wheel,* hands clenched and body entirely strained toward a destination that recedes at the same pace the vehicle advances. Strictly observe the *egomobile code*: ride the bumper of those who mistakenly get in front of you; at each red light, tap your foot impatiently and champ at the bit until the light turns green; at the slightest slow-down, gesticulate, honk, make your displeasure known, etc. Every trip will therefore turn into an opportunity to get carried away and identify with your fantasies of all-powerfulness.

Fast and Furiously Wins the Race

In order to always remain strained toward, *go fast, faster, even faster, ever faster*, not only in your car, but from start to finish of your day. Why fast? It hardly matters. That's not the question. It's a question of charging through life like a bull, head down, toward the red cape of ever-receding goals and desires. The precious principle of *time-lagging-forward* goes usefully hand-in-hand with the *racing principle*. Don't walk, run; don't advance, charge; don't be quick when haste is of the essence, be "speedy" by reflex, even when you shouldn't be. Remember: *speed is the ally of non-vigilance, the guarantee of self forgetfulness*.

There again, you'll profit from the massive support of our speed worshipping society. Everything conspiring to make a healthy slowness impossible, you'll have no trouble being perpetually in a hurry. This continual haste will permit you to gulp down life rather than savor it and thus never garner its substance. Confuse precipitation with rapidity, agitation with efficiency. Once on your way, never think to slow down. The simple fact of making your motions in a less hasty manner could unfortunately promote getting back in touch with yourself. Thus, do not stop, neither rest nor slow down, accelerate even more, compensate anxiety by an ever quicker pace.

Non-Deliberate Living

To promote that forward flight, *do not live deliberately*. Begin by cultivating more irregular daily habits. Eat and sleep any old time, any old way, always too little or too much. That will suffice to institute a psycho-physiological unbalance crucial to non-vigilance.

Live in disorder. Never put an object back in its place, starting with your glasses and car keys. That way you will be, without fail, agitated and irritated each time you need to drive and see clearly.

Put off what you need to do until another day. Above all, don't do it now. Put off everything until tomorrow. That way, you're ensured of being mentally tense and divided. In general, cultivate the indistinct, the almost, the vague. All precision should be forbidden. Let your existence be ruled by the *principle of disorganization*. At home, for example, chores must not be clearly allotted, schedules must be vague, budgets nonexistent, etc. The most elementary aspects of daily life will become a source of unending problems, each family member feeling constantly on guard.

Take care to surround yourself with *conditions hostile to all vigilance*. For example, live with the television and/or radio constantly on while you go about your routine tasks. Let there always be background noise that no one listens to but that is there nonetheless, following the example of the supermarket where, in the aisles, a phantom music floats, lulling the consumers. As greedy as they are harassed, they go about their wanderings without even noticing it.

To feel desperate and stay that way, be an addict of the fax, cell phone, Internet, and other tools that are in themselves practical, yet factors of an ever greater frenzy. In using them without moderation you'll unceasingly be ever more confronted with information you can't assimilate, with the result that your mind will be constantly agitated, gripped by a sensation of saturation. This gorging of facts favors the non-mastery of thoughts, discussed in the next chapter.

Submerged by requests, propositions, solicitations (thanks to the above-mentioned tools), never say no. Accumulate projects, obligations, appointments, etc. This way you'll have the constant sensation of being "swamped."

Along this line, *never do just one thing at a time, always do several things at once*. Routinely eat while playing on the computer's keyboard or watching television; have the phone in one hand while preparing a meal with the other; find a third to slap your child who's been sitting there crying for no reason, and so forth.

By following all these recommendations you'll reinforce the ill effects of the principles essential to the way of non-vigilance: the division principle, the time-lagging-forward principle, the racing principle, etc. You'll thus cultivate a relationship to existence that's, in itself, unfavorable to all practice.

Finally, don't forget to seek support from the comments constantly secreted by the mind as to your exercises along the way. If by chance you get the crazy idea to train yourself in vigilance, above all be vexed and furious when you realize you haven't been present. Ruminate your failure, cultivate spite and bitterness toward yourself. The simplest thing would be to solemnly decide that, starting this very second, you will no longer entertain the merest useless idea and will always give everything your full attention. Thus you will be certain to disappoint yourself. Going from one disappointment to another, you will have quickly renounced all attempts at practice. Deny that your responsibility begins the moment you remember, ends the moment you forget, and that the important thing is to cultivate the intention to not forget. Go from the principle that you will not forget, have forgotten, be apt to forget in the future, and that, consequently, you are intrinsically bad. A kingdom divided against itself can do nothing, therefore you will program your own impotence.

In summary, don't forget that *non-vigilance is the very non-sadhana that will take you away from the goal*. Always start from the principle that the important thing is not now but in a while, later, before. Not *what is* but what was or will be. Maintain the conviction that the present is totally and irremediably defined by the past, never new or open. Live in the certainly that you "know." You will remain, without fail, in a gray and shabby world.

3

I Am Not Therefore I Think

The Non-Mastery of Thought

You must always think. It's every thing; it's the only question. In order not to feel the marvelous life that carries you and roots you, you must think without respite.
— after Charles Baudelaire,
as adapted by the Spiritual Enemy

All the recommendations given in this chapter can be summed up as one: do not see, think. Carefully maintain an incessant, unrelenting mental activity. Never ever let your brain rest. Have no fear. The contemporary context proves extremely favorable to the constant production of useless, parasitic thoughts. You'll therefore have no trouble following your Spiritual Enemy's instructions. In fact, you're following them already. The most you can do is to push the method of functioning that has become natural to you even further.

Think That You Are Seeing, Don't See That You Are Thinking

First of all, remain confused as to the meaning given on the path to the verb "to think." Don't forget that illusion prospers in vagueness, in the more-or-less. Consequently, *establish no distinction between vision, that is to say the conscious use of intelligence, and thought in the sense of the automatic production of useless mental representations.* See no difference between useful thoughts – those with which you prepare an activity, reflect on a matter or simply arrive at conceptualizations that are indispensable to communicating and to human existence; and useless thoughts – those that are mere embroidery, add-ons and add-add-ons, daydreams, fantasies, delusions, rumination … in a word, wool-gathering!

This way, you'll be *certain to think you are seeing, not to see that you are thinking*.

Set Off Smartly on the Wrong Foot

A bad start being a giant step toward failure, it's important to practice the non-mastery of thoughts from the moments you wake up.

When you regain consciousness in the morning, above all don't get up right away. Remain in a half sleep, particularly propitious to cogitating. You'll thus set off on the wrong foot before even having placed it on the floor. Huddle under the covers, picture all your various problems and difficulties. See the day to come as a movie, preferably a disaster film. This process has the advantage of quick efficiency. Each second thus spent in secreting negativity will render you more and more depressed, downtrodden, discouraged. Above all, use every opportunity that presents itself. If you wake feeling physically tired, deny the sensation immediately. Heavily reinforced with thoughts, evoke all the afflictions of fatigue. Be tired of being tired; feel like the victim of the fatigue you are experiencing. Rather than welcoming the sensation of the moment as a given that's part of life's flux, *qualify* it, label it, let all the disagreeable associations linked to the impression of fatigue come to the surface. *Compare*, while moaning internally, today's fatigue to the wellbeing of yesterday and the day before. Tell yourself that this fatigue will never go away; then address all the causes, real or imagined, of this fatigue until an impression of being crushed by the burden installs itself. Put off getting up as long as possible because it could have the unfortunate effect of setting you in motion, activity being the enemy of cogitation.

The ideal would be that you stay cowering under the covers and sink into the vicious circle of a depression consisting of a mass of negative thoughts solidified into paralyzing emotions. It's undoubtedly easier than you think, as you'll be able to verify yourself if you follow the preceding instructions to the letter.

To Think More, Feel Less

If life's call continues to prove the strongest and, despite a prolonged stay in a debilitating limbo, you get up anyway, fear not and go onto the next step.

Once you're up, you need only persist in the dispositions well begun upon awakening. Be careful not to let your attention be drawn to your daily gestures and minor activities such as showering, preparing and eating breakfast, and so forth. Remember that feeling is the enemy of thinking. *To think more, feel less.* In the shower, for example, do not allow the body to fully enjoy the sensation of warm water on the skin.

Although you can't, alas, completely obliterate sensation, it is in your power to render it inoperative as a possible recall to reality simply by taking care not to encourage it by paying attention to it. Sensation doesn't bring you back to what's real unless by your practice you feed it the fuel of consciousness, i.e., your attention. The instruction is thus very clear: When you're in the shower, think. Don't taste your coffee, swallow it mechanically and think. Do not enjoy the simple fact that you feel alive. Think. Avoid glimpsing outside, sticking your head out the window, breathing the morning air: that could have the unfortunate effect of putting you back in contact with sensation. Think. Pay no attention to breathing, to inhaling and exhaling, that ever-available door to feeling. Think. If you have somewhere to go, either on foot, by car or by public transportation, use the time to think again and again. Avoid paying attention to the view; stay immersed in your cerebral universe. If, in the bus or on the subway, for example, your gaze takes in the other passengers, let what your eyes perceive be another opportunity to think rather than see. Judge, compare, label, imagine.

If, When, If Only, Provided That ...

Following these recommendations will allow you to approach the day in a state of mental feverishness particularly propitious to non-progression along the path. You will need to confirm this positioning in such a way that this bad start will indeed evolve into spiritual drowning. In order to take full advantage of what you've acquired, you must capitalize on the different types of thoughts which, in and of themselves, come to you.

Here's how your Spiritual Enemy proposes to proceed: A

very popular category of thoughts is that which relates to activities and tasks to be accomplished. In this case, it's a matter of perverting a legitimate and necessary usage of intelligence to turn it into a factor of dispersion or even panic.

Begin by enumerating all the things you have to do, should have done, don't want to do but must do anyway, etc. Take care to completely confound this mental consternation with organization. Rather than seeing and noting the things to be done one by one, let them rush in upon you like a wave so that you immediately feel submerged. When a task to accomplish comes to mind, take care to follow two rules that will guarantee that you maintain the above-mentioned impression of drowning.

Never do what you have to do right away. Put it off until later, taking care that this "later" remains the vaguest of concepts. Never decide to do such and such a thing at such and such a time of the day. Content yourself with thinking, "I must do this, I must do that," without this meaning that you know when or where. Thus, a horde of thoughts relative to the things to accomplish, and therefore apparently justified, will savagely present themselves from the time you get up until you go to bed, and even pursue you in your dreams.

You will note that the non-mastery of thoughts proves to be inseparable from the non-vigilance previously discussed. Do not forget: disorganization, the cultivation of the vague and the more-or-less are the allies of thought.

The other category of thoughts is that concerning the possible future – "what *might* arrive."

As regards this, the rule is simple: constantly confound possibilities and probabilities. Using a little mental hocus-pocus, let what might happen appear to be what will happen. Let the always-possible present itself as the highly-probable or even the ineluctable. The range of possibilities being almost endless, the mine from which you extract your fears as well as your desires is inexhaustible. Given these conditions, why restrain yourself? Go for it!

The key formula is summed up in two words: "What if … "
Let them become the mantra thanks to which you will be able either to scare yourself or please yourself to your heart's content. Starting with this incantation, give carte blanche to the mind. In order to scare yourself, give your mind the latitude to complete

the magic phrase with the most disquieting possibilities.

What if ... I get cancer?

What if ... my loved ones all die in a car accident?

What if ... the airplane I'm about to board crashes?

What if ... a hurricane destroys my home?

Above all, don't restrict yourself to the single register of fears and other worries. The ideal would be to automatically alternate, using a set of compensations and counterbalances, between the production of fears and that of marvelous possibilities. In order to please yourself, proceed in the same manner, finishing the magic formula with terribly exciting possibilities.

Here are a few examples:

What if I win a bundle in the lottery?

What if I meet the love of my life tonight?

What if a movie producer spots me in the street and offers me a great role in his or her next film?

The efficacy of "What if ... " relies on its magnificently pernicious character: that which is possible is indeed, by definition, not impossible. It's a fact that planes may crash, that entire families perish while driving off on vacation, that a lottery ticket turns a minimum-wage earner into a millionaire, that a malady cuts someone down in his prime, and so forth. It's inside this margin that the mind will most advantageously engulf itself.

Taking recourse uniquely in "What if ... ," however, does not suffice to feed the daily moment-to-moment frenzy for thoughts. Indeed, if you're denied the privilege of tumbling directly into the pathology (hypochondria, paranoia, mythomania, and other states adopted by a triumphant mind), you won't be capable of imagining, from start to finish of the day, either catastrophes or miracles. Thus you risk, in between two attacks of fear or fantasy, accidentally returning to reality. In order to refine and generalize the confusion between possible and probable, to assure it infiltrates every inch of your psyche and pollutes, not occasionally but second after second, your relationship to existence in all instances and without the slightest moderation, you must use, as a tool, *interpretation*.

The recipe is limpid: never stop at the facts, at what you see, and at the objective examination of situations. *Interpret* them in one sense or another. Otherwise put, unrelentingly think of an event by always taking care beforehand to isolate it from the whole. Remember *there are only problems, not situations*. The nature of life is that it incessantly offers situations that eventually call for a response in the form of action.

The mind draws from the material furnished by situations to fabricate problems. The privileged instrument of this fabrication is called "interpretation."

In practice, when faced with any situation, even the most benign, imagine, embroider, dream, proceed to excessive association, come to a too hasty conclusion. If a colleague passes you in the corridor without saying hello, it's obviously because he's got a grudge against you. A registered letter you have to sign for always bears bad news. If your twelve-year-old son flunks math, his professional future will certainly be bleak.

Although the mind feeds on the "problems" it itself fabricates from situations, it can also prosper by secreting positive interpretations. The principle to apply is identical to the preceding one. You only need to change the orientation of the interpretation from the negative to the positive pole. If a woman smiles at you, see this as proof of your irresistible powers of seduction. If your child gets a good mark on her essay, imagine you're already at the cocktail party held to celebrate her Pulitzer Prize. If you get a raise, it's a sign you're one of the "winners" destined to the loftiest summits of the corporate ladder.

Mental cuisine is based on the recipe for the soufflé. Whether it's to fabricate a "problem," or on the other hand to concoct enthusiasm, whether it's a matter of seeing life through dark or rose-colored glasses the principle is always to blow a fact or piece of information out of proportion.

The principle of thought-interpretation being clearly assimilated, you have complete latitude to apply it to all areas, to take it from every angle. The doors to the infernal kingdom are now wide open to you. Here are a few of the roads your Spiritual Enemy invites you to explore.

Mind Network and Radio Cogito

As often as possible take the wide boulevard of day-dreams. Your brain is a fabulous reservoir of fantasies, imaginings and personal mythology. Consequently, dream, or more accurately, *daydream*. Turn your life into your own mind-made movie. Let the cerebral films run uncontrollably until they invade the entire screen of your conscience. Acquire a cosmic satellite dish so you can get the Mind Network; consecrate the better part of your days and nights to flipping from one show to another. Sex, violence, exoticism, heroism, romanticism, nostalgia, disaster films, everything is there. Be captivated by the variety of scenarios that are nourished by your latent fears and desires. Stay tuned day and night to Radio Cogito with its old but still fascinating and unforgettable tunes, its ads, its tempting offers, its announcements, its debates, its permanent commentaries on your own actuality. Radio Cogito and Mind Network even offer you spiritual programs, whether they be forums, discussions ("Is it or isn't it necessary to have a master?") or its great initiatory sagas in which you are the hero – the most unforgettable one being, "My Liberation," a never-equaled fresco now available in 3-D.

To guarantee both the variety and the power of your thoughts, interpretations, daydreams and fantasies, take care to fuel them daily by consuming the news, reading papers and magazines, absorbing information from the television, radio or multimedia. Above all don't neglect that precious aid to your non-practice that's brought to you in profusion each day by our magnificent "entertainment society." The marvelous thing about information is that it stuffs your mind with facts that are often disquieting and usually useless for leading your life here and now. It thus furnishes you with material to perpetually renew agitation, an agitation that, moreover, has been turned into an asset in our culture, which is decidedly beneficial for the Spiritual Enemy.

By virtue of a dogma dictated by the entertainment society, not only can you, but it's your duty to, know all – about the most diverse problems and questions, declined like verbs by an army of media professionals in an unheard of luxury of details, analyses and cross-analyses.

Saint Information's reign constitutes an exemplary victory for your servant, the Enemy. Exemplary in that this compact mass of thoughts, interpretations, presumptions and emotions inappropriately baptized "the News" isn't seen for what it is, but passes, today, for reality itself. The News – notably televised news programs – accomplishes on a planetary scale what the mind accomplishes on the individual level: elements of the whole are arbitrarily chosen and presented as the whole itself, a presentation from which conclusions are drawn; these conclusions then give rise to incessant commentary to the point where the process perpetuates itself into infinity.

Therefore, make a silk purse out of this sow's ear. Gorge yourself on the news until you're ready to pop. Let everything be a pretext to fatten up your mind. "Crazy cow," hoof and mouth disease, the economic crisis, the spectre of unemployment, social conflicts, the greenhouse effect, cloning, religious fanatics, business, etc. Let everything suit you for living in an atmosphere of menace, mistrust, disillusionment, depression. Just as with *"Mind tells the truth,"* don't infringe on the formula *"The news is reality."* Scrutinize the topics, ruminate about them. Your excuse is already there: you are keeping yourself informed. Starting with an ego already naturally on the defensive, you'll end up with a desperate ego, always on guard; political, ecological, social or economic preoccupations serving to confer a status of objectivity to your unconscious's confused terrors. Use these major topics to give a little spice to your life; to scare you and everyone else.

In order to render your fears rustproof, decide you are dispensed from having any real general culture that could inopportunely allow you to step back and gain some perspective on your worries of the moment. Let today's newspaper take the place of any historical context, and let the Arts section of a magazine be as far as your culture goes. Don't in the least take history lessons into consideration. Forget, for example, that your parents or grandparents lived in the climate of the "Cold War," under the Damocles' sword of an atomic holocaust that never arrived. Base everything on the inevitable character of the predominating analyses in order to exclude the unforeseeable, the unimaginable – in other words, life and its infinite creativity. Forget there was a time when no one would have seriously predicted the fall of the Berlin Wall or, on a totally different level and even longer ago, the arrival of two thousand years of Christian domination. Content yourself with being afraid or hopeful – it's the same thing – by relying on the always restrictive and limited logic of the mind.

Confuse "food for thought" with "food for thinking." Take "thought" and "debate" to mean what is only the regurgitation of media nourishment excessively consumed and thus badly assimilated. Let everything furnish a pretext for thinking. When you state an opinion, it should not spring from your own experience but be a quote from your favorite media sources.

Words, Words, Words

From this point on, talk, talk, talk, voicing one's thoughts being a way to fuel them. *Assiduously practice the non-control of conversations*. Discuss, for hours, the rise of extreme right-wing movements, euthanasia, or the situation in the Near East. Speak fiercely about this one, that one, your neighbors, your colleagues, and, why not, the spiritual master and his entourage. Speak, think aloud, pronounce your judgments – there will always be something to say. These marvelously vain discussions, beside the fact that they'll inject even more "reality" into your thoughts, thus solidifying the mental sediment you're ensconced in, will also have the advantage of alienating your own entourage, of rendering you unavailable to your nearest and dearest. For example, pay no attention to the drawing your five-year-old daughter shows you because you're too busy watching a show on children's rights.

Get inflamed, plead causes, argue. Remember: *to turn the path into a dead end, persist in fostering opinions*. Take note of the distinction between "having an opinion" and "cherishing" it. It's inevitable that, as a human being, you have a certain amount of opinions. The simple fact of voting liberal or conservative does not, in itself, promote your non-practice. Thus, the important thing is not having opinions but cherishing them. Attach so much importance to your opinions that you end up confounding yourself with them and feeling it's your mission to defend them tooth and nail. Consequently, be "for," be "against." Apply yourself to having fixed opinions about everything and define your very identity through your relationship to others according to the opinions they have.

Practically speaking, *let identification with your opinions not only justify your emotions, but bedeck them with every virtue.* Let your noble ideas be an unconscious pretext for giving free rein to your most primitive impulses, to your repressed aggression and your dreams of revenge. Kill the partisans of the death penalty with your look; segregate yourself from the racists; violently militate for peace; decide that those who defend abortion and euthanasia don't have the right to live. Do not for an instant tolerate those you deem as intolerant. Scorn and reject, in the name of Christ (or Allah or Jehovah or Buddha), those completely opposed to spirituality. Be ready to torture the tormentors, condemn the judges, oppress the oppressors. You will thus perpetuate the victory of the Enemy, prince of this world, in fuelling the fire of hate on the pretence that you're extinguishing it.

It goes without saying that to place yourself in a coherent manner along this line, you must mistake a battle based on hate for the legitimate defense of values essential to you.

I Think Therefore I See Not

At this stage ask yourself a question that's crucial to your non-practice: the line between *vision*-evaluation and *thinking*-interpretation seeming sometimes fine, how can I be certain to really and truly think rather than see? Thinking, like vision, is accompanied by symptoms that are easily recognizable. Thought, conscious or not, gives rise to the emotions, while vision results in a state of calm. Just as alcohol absorbed beyond a certain level enters quickly into the bloodstream and induces drunkenness, the consumption of useless thoughts allows them to penetrate the body, regardless of its finesse or lack thereof, and induces a state of emotional intoxication that quickly leads you to find yourself in a state of pronounced agitation. Just as the sensation of being drunk indicates non-sobriety, your level of confusion and emotional perturbation is the best indicator at your disposal to verify your persistence in non-vision.

Therefore, react immediately; don't wait for vision to

install itself – it would then be too late! As soon as the first symptoms of vision appear, inoculate yourself with a strong dose of thinking.

Happily, the mechanism of thought works like a set of gears. Once in motion, it is self-fuelling and develops from its own dynamism. There's no need, therefore, to stop yourself from seeing; from immediately thinking a lot; from rousing the rabble of your fantasies, fears and wild imaginings right away. It will be naturally and rapidly self-evident; you need only set the mechanism in motion and authorize yourself to think, if only a little.

Seek first the kingdom of the mind and its injustice; all the rest – the tears and the gnashing of teeth – will be offered as a bonus.

Would you like never to be free from the illusory and infinite meshes of thinking and from the revelry of emotion? If the answer is yes, consume thoughts, just like drug addicts do drugs. See or think, you've got to choose. Thinking has one great advantage in terms of non-practice, it is a drug; the surest way to get "hooked" on one form of narcotic or another and stay that way is to consume it regularly. To perpetuate your dependency, tell yourself, regarding thinking, exactly what the smoker or inveterate drinker tells himself: "One cigarette and I quit"; "Just a glass, one glass … ," etc. Lull yourself with the illusion that, from this moment on, you can control the wild horses of the mind. Most addicts insist they can stop "whenever they want," even though they can't do without the product. Insist, likewise, on the pretension that you can decide to think or not to think, in order to authorize orgies of wool-gathering. The mind resembles a bazaar lined with shops – on the doorstep of each one, there's a merchant who invites you to come inside. Each thought seems urgent and important to you. Be, as regards thinking, like the tourist who enters the shop "just to look around," and leaves with the arms filled with objects that are as useless as they are expensive.

Of course, the harmful effect of a thought depends on the degree of our identification with it. Consequently, *do not see that you think and think that you see which*, in practice, signifies: *don't recognize thoughts as thoughts*. Don't regard them as mental content; don't regard yourself as a subject observing those

objects called thoughts. On the contrary, confound yourself totally with them. Consider them as reality itself and never cast
doubt on them. Establish no distinction between the mind and
the truth. Do not deviate from the axiom: *the truth is what the
mind says*.

Thinking is based on the conviction of knowing, while
vision veers toward the "I don't know." The "I know" is closed;
the "I don't know," open, available. Therefore, you must at all
costs protect yourself from this "I don't know." Be peremptory.
Start from the principle that you saw ... see ... will see. The others think, not you. Don't deny yourself, either, the pleasure of
letting them know. The remark, "You're so stuck in your mind,"
is always effective, it being again understood that the others are
thinking as soon as they don't see things the same way you do.

Once you've laid the foundation, all that's left for you to
do is think. Luckily, the theme of the mastery of thought solicits
very little attention among spiritual seekers who generally rele-
gate it to the realm of meditation exercises completely cut off
from their daily existence. Your thoughts still have some fine
years ahead of them. Dream of awakening, liberation, wisdom,
and think like a log. You'll be suffering for a long time.

Your Spiritual Enemy, being a man of taste and refinement, permits himself, by way of concluding this chapter, to
quote the short prose poem by Charles Baudelaire, called "Get
Drunk," then to share with you his own version. Learn it by
heart, if you want, which will confer a poetic dimension to sabotaging your sadhana.

You must always be drunk. It's everything: it's the only
question. In order not to feel the horrid burden of Time
that weighs upon your shoulders and stoops you towards
the ground, you must get drunk without respite.

But on what? On wine, poetry or virtue, as you like. But
get drunk.

And if sometimes on the steps of a palace, the green grass
of a ditch, in the mournful solitude of your room, you
awaken, the drunkenness already diminished or gone,
ask the wind, the wave, the star, the bird, the clock,

everything that's fleeting, everything that whimpers, everything that rolls, everything that sings, everything that speaks, ask what time it is; the wind, the wave, the star, the bird, the clock will respond: It's time to get drunk! So as not to be slaves martyred by Time, get drunk; get drunk unceasingly! On wine, on poetry or on virtue, as you like.

You must always think. It's everything: it's the only question. In order not to feel the marvelous life that carries you and roots you, you must think without respite.

Think of what? Of the past, the future, about the present, as you like. But think. And if sometimes, on the steps of a palace, the green grass of a ditch, in the blessed solitude of your room, you awaken, the drunkenness of thinking already diminished or gone, ask the mind, the ego, the unconscious, the child within you, everything that foments, everything that avoids, everything that refuses, everything that agitates, ask what time it is; and the mind, the ego, the unconscious, the child within you will respond: It's time to think! So as not to be the sage free of Time, think; think unceasingly! Of the past, of the future, about the present, as you like.

4

The Kouple War

How to Be Done
With the Law of Difference

Ah, the couple ... Your Spiritual Enemy sighs with relief at the very evocation of this relationship in whose heart he prospers, realizes his full potential, becomes twice as creative and gives his all.

What possibilities for illusion, confusion, misunderstandings, perversities, getting lost, lies, dishonesty, dead ends, folly and more. In other words, what sufferings to wallow in until the tragedy hits...

If the Spiritual Enemy feels at home everywhere, the couple is the place he most likes to be. He finds particular pleasure, certainly, at the core of churches, monasteries, ashrams, spiritual communities and other places consecrated to the essential, which he succeeds in reducing to his service; but the pleasure he finds deep within the couple, that fundamental human structure, quintessential relational space, basis of the family and thus all that follows, is unequalled.

The Other? What Other?

First and foremost, a word of advice: *if you're in pain, act as if it had nothing to do with intimacy*. Ignore the fact that, for better or worse, you are your mother's child and therefore in search of intimacy before anything else. Use meaningful words and vast concepts – "spirituality," "awakening," "non-duality," "liberation," "enlightenment," etc. – to deck out and magnify the simple hope of feeling unconditionally loved and thus reassured. As a more or less conscious and successful attempt to recreate our relationship with the very first Other, our mother, the couple concentrates the most powerful desire as well as the profoundest fear. Don't lose yourself in contemplation about it. Imagine the spiritual quest as the pursuit of a special state, hypothetically called "awakening" or "sainthood," in which you will finally stand at a safe distance from relationship, immunized against intimacy, loved and venerated by all. A state in which, untouched by anyone in particular, you will advance through life like the pope in his acclaimed and armored "popemobile" – the bullet-proof car-fortress in which the poor man has to greet the crowds. Therefore, envision the awakened relationship to life as something like the popemobile.

Never imagine that the outcome of the quest could be ultimate intimacy: an intimacy no longer projected toward the exterior – the others – but totally invested within yourself; in the very heart of what you are; in communion with you and thus with others; everyone else essentially no longer sensed as "others" but as forms of yourself. Yes, really, don't be embarrassed by these unusual considerations. See the path as the definitive triumph of your ego. That will help you to sink the couple, to guarantee without a doubt your spiritual failure.

Yes, the couple really is the privileged arena of non-practice, the moment of truth where, the masks torn off, you appear in your terrifying emotional true light: that of a little child perpetually begging for love and ready, in order to attain it, for any kind of manipulation – from sadistic domination to lethal submission, without forgetting seduction, supplication, threats, tyranny, verbal and physical abuse, lies, obsessions and other goodies. Your Enemy just loves the couple where the finer principles are annihilated, where resolutions are broken, where talk is meaningless, where meditation, prayers, mystical ecstasy, intellectual knowledge, exercises and practice are reduced to smithereens under the pressure of *emotional demand*.

He just loves it while at the same time being wary of it.

The truth revealed by the couple proves marvelously negative as long as it's not seen and used as the ideal fulcrum for practice. Your enemy appreciates the fact that within the couple the masks are torn off; because, once torn, the field is wide open to the emotional vampire whose distorted features they've dissimulated. The Enemy relishes seeing the truth unveiled when that consists of unloading the crudest impulses, of giving a green light to all the infantilisms. He's delighted that practice can no longer hold up – except as a reference used to dominate the other ("you should practice!"). He's jubilant that one permits him or herself, within the ramparts of the couple, negative and senseless comportment that one would never indulge in elsewhere. On the other hand, he has a loathsome fear of the rare but always possible reversal of the couple into an instrument of progression. By the very truth its raw light illuminates, the couple constitutes the most efficient aid to spiritual sabotage. Yet, along with the master, it's also potentially the menace to be most dreaded. Where would one be if couples, rather than using the relationship as the ideal arena of identification and emotional outburst, turned it into a space devoted to vision, took it as the opportunity above all others to see each other and to finally stand for one's practice? How dangerous it would be if two human beings, having unfortunately taken it into their heads to practice, took full advantage of each pain experienced in their relationship to clearly see their weaknesses and try to surmount them ...

The Conjugal Armory

Of course, the risk is small. Coexistence can't remain peaceful for long. *The couple is, as it should be, a war.* It must stay that way. The entire purpose of this chapter is to make sure the couple never gets past the stage of perpetual confrontation – more or less latent. Never, but never, let the existence of the next stage, that of collaboration, be suspected. As to the accomplishment of the couple, the stage of communion, it must neither be imagined nor conceived as possible. Confused with fusion, yes, of course. Glimpsed for what it is, a complementary state born of the essential autonomy of each person, no never!

Thus, it's a matter of limiting ourselves to war. Would that this war be bloody, cruel, destructive. Would that it not only permitted you, daily, to treat your commitment to the path with scorn, but also to nip the least whim to practice in the bud by consuming all the energy you might possess. Would that the couple war, like any decent war, whether it be waged with minor skirmishes or brutal bayonet confrontations, kill your self-respect, wipe out your lust for life and even your dignity. Let it be a holocaust that leaves the hearts turned to rubble, the psyches worn out, children permanently damaged.

Let the couple be the fatal finish of your path, the Waterloo of your combat against the mind, the Custer's Last Stand of your spiritual retreats and resolutions.

The entire role of life and truth contained in the couple must be detoured, perverted to the advantage of non-practice and blindness. This is what your Enemy heartily wishes for you.

Thus is the sense of the present chapter and the advice it offers you.

The Splendid Solitude of the Self

A primary strategy, a very simple one, consists in *avoiding the couple*. Although less promising in terms of degradation, violence and diverse torments, this solution has the merit of almost guaranteeing a tranquil non-progression. What you'll lose in opportunities to seek satisfaction in refusal, to react on the spur of the emotion and abdicate all dignity, you will gain in illusion. If, in cooking yourself up à la carte a spiritual life that's made of blessed solitude, profound meditations, peaceful walks, with the fewest possible disturbances for the ego, you succeed in existing more or less calmly, you've won the bet. It's understood that you will not opt for one form or another of institutionalized religious life. Instead of establishing yourself in sublime solitude, you would quickly find an affective bone to pick in your relationship with the community, the abbot, obedience, etc.

The various traditions, well aware of the temptation for people with mystic propensities to use the monastic life as a means to avoid relationships, have unfortunately organized community life as a field of ceaseless ego frictions. What with vows of poverty, stability, obedience, chastity, your ego would quickly suffocate! Consequently, don't do anything serious; make sure you avoid any kind of precise involvement. Be neither monk nor cloistered nun with responsibilities to your order and your community, nor man nor woman completely invested in family life. Opt for some vague-in-between, propitious to every sort of illusion. Arrange the most tranquil existence for yourself with the fewest possible disturbances. May your spiritual quest turn into seeking for the niche, a cozy hiding place. Mistake being conveniently left alone for the peace that passeth comprehension. See your neurotic obsession with independence as a manifestation of non-dependence. In other words, live alone.

Consider the question settled once and for all, and cast a politely condescending glance at "all those couples who fight." If necessary, dispense advice and counseling to them. You will always find the naïve, the romantics, and the lost who see in your old-maid's – or diehard bachelor's – rationalizations the expression of a spiritual accomplishment that's out of the ordinary. Take our Catholic bishops as role models – they who from the toes of their pontifical slippers preach about sexual and family difficulties with an authority born of the absence of experience. Look deeply down on that which you wouldn't have the strength to take upon yourself. Of course, you've got to be the first one to believe this. If possible, develop an entire theology around your solitude. Grow lyrical about the "desert," the "retreat," the virtues of "silence." Don't become a monk but quench yourself with readings on the monastic life, on desert fathers, hermits and other anchorites. Cultivate mystical states, contemplations and transports, all the while avoiding to ask yourself what would be left of your ecstasy if you were faced with a spouse's changing moods at the same time as you wiped one child's bottom while another child demanded to be told a story … Opt for radical teachings without concession, such as, "there is no one … ," and so on and so forth. Of course, it will be necessary for you to win on all sides. Do not think that this strategy assumes that you renounce the pleasures of the flesh. If you don't succeed in simply repressing your impulses on the grounds of celibacy – which would also be perfect from the point of view of non-practice but is not within the grasp of just anyone – leave them free rein by giving them a thick coating of tantrism.

Live alone, don't let anyone else arrive and mess up your nice little meditation corner but, at the same time, practice "non-dependent," "in the moment," sexual relations. Never get involved; consume while taking care to travesty as liberty that

The Kouple War   67

which is mere complaisance. You'll have no trouble finding partners, since ashrams, retreat centers and spiritually oriented workshops are rife with men and women seeking affection. The more aloof, deep, mysterious you will appear, the more attractive you'll become. The ideal would be to attain the status of itinerant instructor, preaching liberty from one continent to another with a woman and/or man in every port. Your overwhelming fear of intimacy will thus easily pass as detachment and your refusal to get involved as fidelity to something greater than yourself.

In resumé, *the essential thing is to avoid intimacy*, the core of our humanity and the testing ground of the path. Be neither intimate with another human being – you'll see how, with a little perseverance, it's easy to feel very advanced as soon as there's no one around to bother you at any moment, day or night – nor intimate with God, it being understood that, with the latter, you will fabricate an imaginary intimacy.

The nice thing about God is that he won't use your toothbrush, will absent Himself without a fuss when you want to be left alone, and doesn't have bad breath at seven o'clock in the morning.

To entrench yourself into your own sweet world as if it were a fortress to protect you from life, it's important not to doubt. The couple being likely to introduce, on a daily basis, corrosive doubt about your certitudes and mystical-spiritual accomplishments, you must therefore avoid it. Avoiding a committed couple relationship will allow you, at the same time, to avoid children and a family, another testing ground for transformation.

If, nevertheless, you don't succeed in steering clear of the couple, fear not. Day after day, instant after instant, it will give you countless opportunities for non-practice. Devil forbid that you succeed in using the couple as a tool for progression. At very little risk, therefore, you'll gain a multitude of probable benefits concerning failure on the path! Consequently, there's no cause for regret. *If you can't avoid the couple, you can still avoid the relationship.*

Therefore, launch yourself blindly into the adventure of partnership with, as your only preparation, your expectations, fears, fantasies and all the lies spread on the subject by a narcissistic culture.

The Other? Never Heard of Him!

Begin by maintaining, without question, a romantic and fusionist vision of relationships. Anchor yourself in a false perspective; attack the question from the wrong angle right away.

The key formula, the mantra, that will accompany you from one end to the other of your non-progression in this matter is the following: *the other is not different.* And if s/he is, there's been a mistake. S/he must not be. S/he must be like me. This is the basis on which to found everything. You, like all of us, have never completely recovered from the shock, felt more or less early on, of discovering that Mommy wasn't a projection of yourself but someone else. That there were two of you, not one. You've denied it, refused it, repressed it, and have never stopped fighting the evidence since.

Very good, continue. Let it be the refusal itself that pushes you along "the path to wisdom." Seek non-duality. To pursue false non-duality, the Kouple is the very best avenue to take.

What you need to seek is that which, in fact, you've been looking for all along: *an other who is not an other while being other just the same.* That is the basis of the illusion of love you must continually feed. This quest for "an other not-other being other just the same" permits you, right off the bat, to turn the couple into a myth, to make an absolute of a reality that's so precious and important, certainly, but nevertheless relative.

Along these parameters, *the couple becomes the Kouple.* Note that, here again, our culture proves highly advantageous. Its conception of human love being founded on the romantic ideal, it never focuses on the couple but exclusively on the Kouple, either in the positive sense (extolling of the "love story") or, more and more, in the negative sense (cynical protection from and avoidance of relationships due to the suffering born of the inevitable failure of the Kouple project). The vision of love, that same and sempiternal combat, can be exalted or disillusioned, the latter simply being the reaction to the failure of the former. Everything happens for the worst in the best of all possible vicious circles because the starting point always proves to be false.

The Womb-man Is the Future of the Man-tra

Turn the above into another absolute right away. Let him or her never simply be the other but the Other, the imaginary figure of accomplishment of yourself.

Women, turn man into your Man-tra, the answer, the goal, the happy end of the story, prince charming; this will naturally lead you, the Man-tra disappointing you when he proves to be only a man, to turn him into the obstacle, the monster, the useless, the grain of sand in the machinery of the omnipotent maternal, the bad father always too present or not present enough.

Men, turn woman into your Womb-man, the future of mankind, the horizon, the better half and other foolishness which, the Womb-man disappointing you when she proves to be only a woman, will naturally lead you to turn her into the obstacle, the witch, the bad mother who loves you too much or not enough.

From the very beginning of the relationship, therefore, expect all, and even more, from the other. This positioning, though highly varied in its repercussions and manifestations, is fundamentally simple: from the other, you ask nothing more than all. If you feel something is missing, it's up to the other to provide it. The miracle cure for any need is him or her. Unsatisfied or paid in full, frustration is guaranteed because the need in question cannot be fulfilled by another, whoever s/he is or can be. Note carefully that dissatisfaction is guaranteed even in the case of success, which is the marvelous thing about refusing difference.

Let's admit, though the hypothesis is improbable, that, setting aside your unconscious fascinations and getting past the greater part of your emotional immaturity, you succeed in living with another who really is complimentary to yourself; the simple fact of not questioning the need to feel fulfilled, and thus expecting from your spouse what s/he can't possibly provide, will keep you in a state of latent dissatisfaction, of dependence and fear. *The success of the real relationship will be dimmed, if not completely extinguished, by the ineluctable failure of the imaginary relationship. The inevitable failure of the Kouple will undermine the possible success of the couple.* Consequently, expect, insist, depend, establish the relationship under the sign of need; let the other's attitude be the condition of your fulfillment. Be, from the start and once and for all, perfectly unreasonable in your expectations. You will thus guarantee yourself frustration and disenchantment. In fact, for the few unions presenting real difficulties, there are numerous relationships in themselves viable, but sabotaged, day after day, thanks to this false perspective. All the errors, all the ulterior strayings, will flow from that fundamental aberration: expecting from the other not to be another. *Build your affective life on the misunderstanding of the Kouple, fusion of two halves separated by mistake. Do not conceive of the couple, that association of two people who mutually support one another in order for each one to pursue his or her distinct path.*

In your capacity as great pretender on the path, you have the advantage of being able to add spiritual germs to the Kouple virus already injected by society. Whitewash every encounter with a thick coat of religious-initiatory romanticism. See every call of nature and unconscious fascination as gift-wrapped in ideally rosy tissue paper. You don't fall in love, you find your soulmate, your alter-ego, who has surged from past lives. You're not screwing with somebody, you're engaged in a tantric partnership. See signs, everywhere, correspondences, messages from above that signify the magnificence of the crush you've just developed. Avoid all sobriety, stress lyricism. Sublime, definitely sublime – let that be your motto. Cover an innocent little attraction to a nice pair of buns with an erotic-initiatory peplum, especially if the thing has begun at an ashram, a meditation session, a workshop, etc. Thus, as was mentioned above, centers and ashrams can prove to be great places for picking up people and for romantic exaltation. Mystical loves, tantric transports – don't deprive yourself. Under the Indian banyan trees, the palms of Provence, it's *spirituality, sex and sun!*

Here, incidentally, is an excellent way to sabotage a retreat: from the very first day, keep a lookout for a potential soulmate. Once an attraction has automatically installed itself, spend the greater part of your time fuelling it. In the refectory, during teachings, right on to meditation, seek the other with your eyes. Follow him or her like a puppy, beg for his or her attention. Having arrived with the express intention of finding yourself, even of consecrating yourself to the ultimate, find yourself, quick as a wink, mired in a passion for someone. Above all, make a point to alert the master, to make him endorse your momentary desire. Meet your paramour on Friday, reach second base on Saturday, and on Sunday solicit the master's blessing for this providential union that will necessarily be sublime because it was born on sacred ground. Above all, pay no attention to your guru if he seems to show the slightest reserve as regards your future together. He should give his blessing and then zip his lip. "Shut up and deal us a benediction," that's the silent injunction your Spiritual Enemy suggests you address to the Spiritual Friend.

It will, of course, be to your advantage to precipitate things, to go onto a sexual relationship right away without taking the time to get to know each other and become friends. *Consume first, construct later.* Get involved in a relationship, head lowered like a bull charging the red cape, with no sense of perspective or reflection. Repress whatever doubts and uncertainties may arise; reinforce yourself by compensating them with quotations from the teaching and romantic-spiritual rationalizations.

Rationalizations and quotations suppose that you spend a fair amount of time talking. All right, then, talk, talk, talk. Drown the relationship in a deluge of words always pronounced on the basis of declared or latent emotion. Don't talk a little, in a deliberate way, in order to express and share. Talk a lot until you achieve total confusion. Better yet, talk by phone. Using and abusing this instrument is highly effective for keeping the relationship a mental image, confining it to the head and the emotional magma generated by thoughts. The reign of the cell phone with its possibilities for intrusion any time, anywhere, favors even more these dislocated dialogues. Don't forget that *if Love is blind, it's also deaf*, particularly through the intermediary of the phone. Therefore, telephone 'til you drop. You can't see each other, look into each other's eyes, feel each other, thus imagination has all the latitude. In this manner, give the priority right away to the virtual couple; that's to say always and forever, the Kouple.

Once so engaged in the dead end street of the Kouple, you will be wonderfully positioned for a cruel voyage, destination disaster. It's important, nevertheless, that you persevere in these dispositions and avoid awakening yourself, even a little, at whatever stage of the relationship. To accomplish this, *the essential thing is clinging to the Kouple ideal* without ever questioning it and thus risking to mature from Kouple to couple.

Has Your Heart One Me?

To begin with, at the start of a life with someone else, as soon as a difference seems to appear, deny it. Please, hide that other that just should not be ... The other being the Other, the man being the Man-tra and the woman the Womb-man, any dissemblance would be strictly fortuitous. *In the kingdom of the Kouple, the non-same has no claim; there is only the won-me/one-me.* Does a disagreement threaten on the horizon? Could one say that the other has ceased to want exactly what you want when you want it? That's an error, nothing really, nonsense. But, aside from that, everything is fine, just fine. From denial to denial – slight, repressed unease to small, unspoken disappointment – you'll find yourself more and more undermined by a dull discomfort as you begin to see the unnamable, "the horror, the horror" as Joseph Conrad would say: the other who I believed to be the Other, not entirely one me nor entirely an other and who won me and one me, that Other is nothing, after all, but an other ...

Maintain this stage of denial as long as possible. When this position ceases to be tenable, when the evidence of the difference can no longer be denied, go onto the next stage, that of bitter and virtuous disappointment. The underlying logic is simple and supposes that you remain in search of the Kouple rather than the couple: at no time question the initial postulate, that's to say your hope of an Other, Man-tra or Womb-man, mandated by God to fill the need in you; this hope remains totally legitimate from your point of view. But, at present, you have the admirable humility to admit you were wrong. S/he wasn't the right one, that's all! Let's just admit it – the other, the infamous, the villain who odiously betrayed you, abused your good faith, making you believe, the monster, that s/he was indeed the Other, the Man-tra, the Womb-man, while being nothing more than another, a woman, a man ... What a lousy trick! You have every reason to feel outraged: I believed ... *you made me* believe ... that you were no different, but, *oh the horror, the horror, you are*! To the extent that you have put the master, despite himself, in the middle of all this, you have there an excellent excuse for holding him responsible: how could he have directed you into this dead end street? Is he then as deprived of compassion as all that? Didn't he see the error, the lie? If, having discerned it, he didn't warn you, it's because he failed in his responsibilities; and if he saw only smoke, is he then truly a master? In short, whatever the case, he is wrong. Blame him then to your heart's content. To the amorous injury will therefore be added, quite opportunely, the spiritual injury in your relationship with the being who is supposed to guide you on the path.

The Cross of the Kouple

All right, you made a mistake, someone deceived you, you were blind but now you see clearly ... Draped in the dignity of the *victim*, you are now faced with two possibilities, equally fruitful from the perspective of non-practice.

The first possibility: you stay in the relationship in the role of virtuous spouse and wait for the other one to change. This position doesn't lack panache. It allows you to suffer in a righteous fashion. There is a wonderful pose to adopt and perfect, that of the *irreproachable spouse crucified on the Kouple cross.* Your entire spiritual course of action, as well as your therapeutic "work," can thus revolve around one marvelously unsolvable point: you are unhappy because of the other who doesn't change, who stubbornly persists in being the other when s/he should be the Other.

This well in place, you need only utilize therapy sessions to complain about the spouse, and interviews with the master or spiritual guide to deplore that s/he "doesn't practice." More or less, clearly expect that the path produces a miracle – that's to say, transforms the other into the Other, leads him or her to see, feel, think and react as you do, at long last. Thus, basing your hopes on this transformation of the other into the Other has the advantage of being totally vain. Disappointment guaranteed ... With a little luck, you'll manage to lose what little faith you still had in this master who did not tell the other how important it was for him or her to change, did not oblige him/her, in the name of obedience and devotion, to "love" you. To stay in the relationship is therefore a promising possibility, the equally interesting alternative being to leave, your mistake admitted, to go in quest of the "Right One," the veritable Other who, this time, will be the One. This course of action will necessarily be fruitful in terms of non-practice since it cannot succeed.

Thus fixated on the legitimacy of your desperate quest for the Other, take care never to blame your expectations and to avoid all questions about the way you function on the intimate level. Multiply idylls, experiences and attempts, more or less quickly aborted, at living with someone; but, above all, *learn nothing*. Your non-practice will thus benefit from the law of repetition: having left one relationship to avoid a problem, you will find yourself confronted by the next relationship, the unconscious perfectly willing to let you attract, like a magnet, the same challenge though with a different face. You need only to never blame yourself, to situate the fault in the other, and, thus justified, to take a tangent. You'll sail from disappointment to disappointment until you reach bitter disenchantment. It may then be a good idea to compensate with spiritualizing rationalizations: "in the end, I was made for the solitary life," "one is always alone on the path," "my commitment and devotion are such that no one is capable of living with me," etc.

In Praise of a Constricted Life

If, nevertheless, you stay, that will be the occasion to use a vast range of *avoidance strategies* in the very heart of the relationship.

Begin – always and forever for that's the key to perpetuating failure – by stubbornly ensconcing yourself in the mad logic of the Kouple. The more savagely this possibility is attacked by the real, the more you need to hang on. *The surest way to compromise your couple is to constantly measure it against the Kouple*. That's why the state called "amorous" is, and must remain for you, the criteria, the relational health barometer. You must, even after months and years, find it abnormal not to feel tipsy, exalted, transported, besieged, entranced. Consider it a sign of relational failure that the eyes of the other/Other, that mirror in which you contentedly admire yourself and laugh to find yourself so attractive, are not those blissful primal waters. In short, if you cease to be captivated, absorbed, everything is wrong. The fascinated are fatigued? It's because Love has been exhausted. It's a known fact, the Other is there to make you feel vast, profound, transcendental. S/he is your supplier of vertigo, the image on glossy paper or the closed-circuit video you use to masturbate your soul. The Other's function consists of taking the conventional poses of Love to fill you with the state of grace, that sublime fusion celebrated in all the songs.

From this point on, ensure that s/he no longer excites you enough, no longer stimulates that sublime itch. See him or her as flat, dull, in a word, worn out like an old video too often played. Have you sometimes seen yourself as petty, mean, narrow-minded, or even ridiculous through the other's eyes? Does excitement occasionally give way to irritation? Now, that should not be and must be considered abnormal. In this domain, as in all the others, society is your ally because the only image it conveys is that of the Kouple, diffused until one is sick of it in various magazines, novels and shows. Nothing but passion, only fascination! How can you be entranced by Love and stay that way? What strategies, games, tricks and artifices should you use in order, at all costs, to maintain the sacrosanct thrill? ... This is the contemporary preoccupation you need to make your own. *Let your thoughts be quotations* – from tabloids– *your emotions, imitations* – of novels, soap operas and the poorly-named "reality" shows – *your actions, caricatures* – caricatures of caricatures staged by all the current representations of Love.

Sex, Lies and Ego Video

Of course, the cult of that thrill is tightly bound to the question of the couple's sexual relations. The Enemy, just like the Spiritual Friend, is very much interested in your sexual life to the extent that it's a highly accurate barometer of your interior positioning.

Though far from being the unique ground that permits your imagination to gambol wildly, sexual life nevertheless provides an excellent opportunity for non-practice. Let your sexual life, within the Kouple, be modeled by the ambient criteria and discourses – nothing less than torrid, glamorous, extreme, etc.

There again, to persist in the way of the Kouple, take the exactly opposite course of that of the couple. Invest everything in the mechanics of Desire, with a capital D like Deity – that value riveted to the Kouple – and ignore simple desire, which belongs to the couple. The process of maturing from Desire into desire is one of the most reliable signs of the passage from Kouple to couple. In the way of the couple, the sexual relation unceasingly simplifies itself. In proportion to the deepening of intimacy, it becomes more and more evident, less and less phantasmatical. It's no longer a question of the partners perpetuating challenges and needing to prove anything to each other, but of offering themselves the gift of an encounter between two intrinsically equal human beings. In the way of the Kouple, on the contrary, everything is stakes, strategy, tension, pursuit of an ideal imposed by a neurotic culture. An ideal that, sexually, finds its expression in the cult of Desire. You must therefore pursue this dead end. The head stuffed with images presented by the media, *start with the principle that desire must be Desire, sex, Sex, and launch yourself in the logic of obligatory eroticism.* Excitement, excitement and even more excitement. Let everything stay on the surface and, more and more, in the head. Make a big deal about the body in its capacity as the docile performer in your most torrid, mental scenarios, provided that the heart and inner presence play no part in your sexual life.

Take the dead end street of "ever more," the road of fantasy; give priority to the forward flight of the "new" and "never before seen." You will thus be certain, sooner or later, to run into a wall, the wall of the mind, with the hope that the relationship will crash.

The stage where, in the Kouple, the sexual relationship seems to have reached its peak, is a moment of truth. There lies the possibility to start quitting the Kouple logic to engage oneself in that of the couple. Deepening the relationship goes hand in hand with a different kind of sexuality. Of course, you must avoid this possibility at all costs or, on the contrary, take advantage of it to rebound even further in the vertigo of the Kouple.

At this stage there are three options available to you. The first, an easy one, consists of extracting yourself from the relationship in order to go, once more, in search of the Right One with the usual erotic guarantee, valid for a few months. The second, which does not exclude going onto the third, is woven with explorations, bypasses and wanderings, in themselves totally conventional and utterly predictable, but extremely audacious to your eyes: you will seek to rekindle the sexual vivacity of your shaky Kouple with the help of a variety of artifices. Let fantasy compensate your relationship's fatigue. You can use the classic hardware, all kinds of accessories, objects, cassettes, underwear and gadgets on sale in specialty shops. Little does it matter what props you use provided they provoke the fantasy, and that everything takes place more and more in the mind. *Anything will do, provided the pretended intensification of the sexual relationship is a way for you to defer and if possible altogether avoid intimacy.* Build, between you and your partner, a wall of fantasies, inventions, scenarios, images, representations drawn from the sources where they proliferate, which is to say everywhere: city walls, TV and movie screens, paper dubbed "glossy," the chic, shocking books that could all be entitled, *The Sexual Life of My Mind,* and so on. In order to avoid seeing and touching the other, just as you avoid being seen and touched by him or her, in order not to plunge in but to skim along the surface, concentrate, logically enough, on the décor. Situate each love scene in a different place. Explore your home. Have sex on the kitchen table, in the basement, on the stairs, in the shower stall, the garage, the tool shed, the laundry hamper, the closet, the doghouse, seated on the toilet ... And why not, oh delight of transgressions, in the meditation room, for want of a church – if, as a true pretender on the path, you've made one wallpapered with photos of your favorite sages. This testing of every nook and cranny will allow you to hold the show over and to always push back the moment of truth when it will be necessary for you to be together, one on one. As concerns the sexual non-relationship, the way of the scenario is also a sure bet. To avoid all risk of intimacy, turn your coitus into theatre. Flee the simple, the obvious, the plain; cultivate the complex, the exaggerated, the gaudy. Thinking you're demonstrating audacity, originality, creativity, offer the conventional, predictable, repetitive. The scenarios are well known, play and replay them with their oldest clichés until you are sick of them. Here are a few great classics, sure hits of nonconformist conformity and obligatory sex: the doctor (male or female) – get hold of a lab-coat, eventually a few instruments and an examining table ... ; the hooker and john – props available everywhere; the shepherd and shepherdess – the trick here is to find a haystack; a little less practiced but within everyone's budget is the butcher (again male or female) – the lab-coat can be used again if you add a few red stains, and you'll also need a hunk of raw meat ... Note, in passing, that, in the choice of scenarios, women tend to give more of themselves than do the male consumers.

If you find these practices, that have become as common as the cell phone, repugnant; if your delicate sensibility is rebuffed by this vulgar filth; if you wouldn't do *"That"* for a billion dollars, you can fall back on the tantric arsenal which is much in vogue in spiritual circles. Leave to the poor souls lost in samsara the usual porno fuelled by Internet or cable television; adorn yours with imagery and an exotic vocabulary come from afar. *Don't screw banally but tantrically.* Let your sexual relations be no longer an encounter but an exercise, or better yet, an erotic-spiritual performance, the exploits in the wings of the great practitioner that you are. Retain your sexual energy, twist and turn every which way as the manuals of posture like the *Kama Sutra* indicate, breathe this way, that way, don't breathe at all, provided it's under a cloud of incense and a new age symphony or some mournful synthesizer is playing in the background. There again, the essential thing is that the apparatus prevents the simple relationship from being laid bare.

Once all these options have been exhausted, why not as a last resort call on partner swapping, on group sex, which has certainly become dated since the '70s but is still in use by couples who have run out of resources.

Try anything except offering yourself the capacity to risk intimacy. By following the preceding suggestions, you'll have done the impossible: you'll have been brazen without ever being brave; you'll have "exposed" yourself in the most unexpected postures and contexts without ever daring to be truly naked.

Of course, the third possibility, commonly practiced and highly convenient for its modalities, is still open to you. It consists of the pure and simple suspension of all sexual life inside the Kouple. Of all the strategies your Enemy has suggested, this one proves to be the most commonly practiced – you'd be surprised at the number of couples existing this way – and the most durable. It has the advantage of favoring an inexorable drying out, an aridity woven of the unspoken, and frustrations resulting in a relational dead end. The principle is obvious: since he or she is not, after all, the Other, since he or she no longer blows you away in the orbit of Desire, well then, it's high time for punishment. I punish you, you punish me, we punish each other. Sex, with a capital S, proves a dead end? Let's abandon it without considering the possibility of sex. End of playtime, goodbye springtime and its scents, let's enter the long and sinister winter of the discontent Kouple. The important thing, once again, is to avoid the couple. The nice thing about escaping through Sex or non-sex is that either form of avoidance eventually dries up the couple.

Above all, don't speak about the vanishing of sexual intimacy. *The sexuality of the couple owes it to itself to disappear discretely*, like that, as if nothing had happened, without threats or condemnation, just a prolonged absence that, in the end, is instituted without saying a word. Let sex be the missing member of the household, installed between the couple like a wall of silence, a thick coating of the unspoken, a hollow resentment, an uncrossable line of demarcation. At this stage it would be opportune to rationalize your frustration by religious considerations. Thanks to the Devil, you'll have a hard time finding, in the diverse religions and spiritual traditions infested by the ideal, a simple and healthy rapport to sexuality. Christian neurosis, like Hindu Puritanism, to name only two great classics in this genre, will furnish you – from the mouths of uncontested sages or saints whose words on this subject nevertheless remain somewhat biased – with all the necessary justifications: taming of the flesh and the exaltations of chastity, the ideal of spouses living as "brother and sister," the denunciation of the "loss of energy," the loss of sperm seen as worse than the loss of blood, and other doubtful developments. Just as it's possible for you to deck the shriveling away that goes along with your life as an old maid or a die-hard bachelor in the apparel of "solitude," don't hesitate to disguise the intimate misery of your Kouple with the masks of "detachment" and "maturity."

Magnified by mysticism or simply silenced, the sexual desert is very useful in that you will get evermore-ideal mileage to the gallon out of it, as well as virtuous causes to defend against a background of latent violence. It's also highly probable that this will lead you, when the time for reaction comes, straight to conjugal infidelity, an old but still excellent recipe for avoiding any risk of deepening the relationship, of discovering desire, of moving from Kouple to couple.

Gone with the Way

These foundations well laid, your Spiritual Enemy proposes that you further refine non-practice at the heart of the marvelous testing ground called the Kouple.

Let's recapitulate: it's understood that the couple can never be anything but the Kouple: the unique objective of living with someone is to render me, myself, happy, a happiness as imagined by the ego and the mind, not one that would help me, through frictions and irritations, to mature toward real intimacy. My relation to the other is, therefore, nothing more than an *expectation, a constant need that s/he behaves as I wish. Not I am a husband, but I have a wife. Not I am a wife, but I have a husband.*

From that point on, if, for eventually the better and above all for the worse, both of you insist that you're "committed to the path," don't hesitate to distort this engagement and use it against each other. *Use the Way as an avant-garde weapon in the continual and bloody Kouple war.* Justify your denial of the other as the other with a raft of quotes from the teaching. Strew your domestic scenes with wise words judiciously chosen to do the most damage, to make the other feel guilty and to create discord in all good conscience.

"You're not in communion with me ... You're not here and now ... You don't practice ... You could at least accept me as I am ... You have no compassion ... You never give me the right to ... ," etc. Thus turn teaching into a towel you throw in the other's face. Once the vocabulary of the Way is used up, you can fill it out with expressions derived from therapy: "There now, you're projecting ... That's your truth, mine is different ... You're so childish ... You're wallowing in your emotions ... That's acting out... ," etc.

Once you've reached this point, it could be a profitable idea, in order to poison things a little more and fuel the magma, to involve the master or spiritual guide. Allude, in a fit of emotion, to indications eventually received during talks with your Spiritual Friend. Evoke his or her comments, especially if they seem to concern, however little, the other, that odiously non-Other. The results are guaranteed. "He said ... "

Note that in proceeding this way you hit two birds with one stone: by miring yourself in emotional blindness you hurt the other, and you commit blasphemy.

Especially during domestic scenes, the reference to teaching can also be usefully established as a rampart against the relationship in everyday life.

Me, I'm the Way, the Truth, and the Life

Although the strategy of at-home teaching is applicable to both sexes, it is more suited to men who will find in it a way to compensate for the fear women inspire in them. Tyrants, fanatics, fundamentalists and dictators of all types are always, under their façade of power, terrified creatures. Domination, physical and mental, is the most ancient of parodies adopted by aging little boys to control the unpredictable, maternal Medusa.

Therefore, men, dominate, diminish, be violent ... Make it your habit, sirs, to play the guru of your couple. Rather than living the teaching silently, talk about it loudly. *Don't discuss things with your wife, preach. Don't converse, teach.* This positioning, ever so efficient to maintain your illusions and perpetuate the cold war between you, is easy and practical: You're afraid of the other, intimacy scares you? Very well, the best ways not to face your fear, to deny and compensate it, are called violence and domination. Spiritual teaching can prove to be a forceful instrument of domination. Adopt the following postulate and never again deviate from it: you are the one who knows, faced with another who does not know. You're "advanced in the Way," the other is a debutante. You see clearly, the other is lost in the shadows. You've "accomplished a lot of work," the other is fumbling about – at this point, you can always concede that, certainly, you still have a ways to go on the condition that the basic affirmation according to which you are nevertheless "evolved," or at any rate *more* than she, is never questioned. From that point on, be peremptory, dry, biting. Use and abuse teaching to diminish the other at every opportunity. Show her the extent to which she "doesn't practice," "doesn't understand," "doesn't see," etc. Downgrade your partner with great slabs of quotations and other saintly words pronounced in acid tones. Domestic tyrants have existed for ages; *the reference to the Way, introduced at the heart of the Kouple, invented the dharma-domestic tyrant, the conjugal guru, Father-Practice.* Not out-of-place complexes, untimely humility: you are (at least in your own home) the Way the Truth and the Life, and no one can get to the master without going through you. You are, unto yourself, the Church, the inquisitor, the executioner.

This position will be most advantageously exploited if you seduce a young recruit who's impressed by your aura of "senior." Put on your best show as he who understands all and is going to take care of everything. Act as if you really believe this – while knowing deep down inside that it's all a hoax which will encourage division in you and push you to flee ever further forward. Consistent with the Kouple logic and the fantasy of the Other as a response to what's missing, this strategy guarantees disappointments, bitterness and the gnashing of teeth. The more your partner glimpses the awful truth – that is, that you are fallible – the more you must entrench yourself in your position, be intractable and odious, until the break-up that, with all its debris, will come to compensate your efforts.

Note that this game takes two players. In order to subjugate, you need a partner whose unconscious strategy consists of playing the role of the subjugated. Count on your unconscious to attract someone with whom you will be able to indulge yourself to your heart's discontent. If the personal ads in the spiritual magazines were stripped of their veneer, they would resemble those published in so many weeklies, even the most respectable: "Idealistic young woman seeks pitiless husband-master to inflict deserved punishment in the form of teaching"; "Man, terrified by women, seeks submissive slave to humiliate at will under the guise of teaching." Following this logic, do everything to control the course the other takes. Dictate how she is to proceed, with which lama, swami, collaborator she will speak, what type of therapy she must undergo and with which particular therapist. Demand, of course, that the other tells you all about the course she takes, keeps nothing to herself. Refuse her the right to a secret garden, always in the name of the Kouple and its transparency. Put the other on report: she will be obliged to give you a full accounting of each session with the master, every revelation on the path. She must recount every retreat in detail. Turn yourself into the savage supervisor of her therapy and the supreme authority of her sadhana, the master being nothing more than a convenient reference to justify your outbursts.

In fact, *every aspect of communal and familial life must transform itself into savage therapy*, into a group dynamic in which you are the uncontested leader, the harsh, indefatigable critic of the projections and infantilisms of your near and dear, the implacable prosecutor of the deviations of the other, the others.

Tell her when and how to meditate, pray, exercise. If the other shows no great signs of resistance to your abuse of power, go even further and instigate, in the heart of the Kouple and of the family – in such a way that the children, if children there are, can really feel the pressure – a set of draconian rules. Drastic diets, obligatory fasting, severely controlled entertainment, prohibited subjects of conversation, and so forth. Turn your home into a police state, a totalitarian regime in which you are the Stalin, a banana republic in which you're the military leader, all that in the name of the Teaching Party, the Mao-Guru, the Big Night Liberation. In this superb genre, the ashram will become the reform school where you expedite the other when necessary. Note that zen sesshins (intensive sitting sessions) can provide a suitable gulag.

If you're in the role of the subjugated, be docile, beatifically servile. Idealize the other to the point that you let him control you body and soul. As soon as your spouse-instructor-mentor-initiator-therapist opens his august mouth, drink in his words and, above all, don't say a word. Constantly go on the principle that he is always "so much more advanced, evolved, mature ... " The error is you, the truth the other.

Let's specify, once more, that this manner of proceeding, if it admirably suits the male, can also be advantageously adopted by the confirmed harpy, the "Mother" fighting for control with Father-Practice.

The Unbearable Lightness of Man-tra

Women have, nonetheless, more specific strategies such as what follows.

Understand, first of all, that in the Kouple war, your advantage, ladies, is, in the end, considerable: every man had a mother whose moods, at one time, set the rhythm of his own and determined his affective make-up. Having disengaged himself from his mother's apron strings only to entangle himself in yours, he is, *a priori*, behind all his airs, decidedly more vulnerable to your interior fluctuations than even he believes. The force, in fact, is with you, the power is in your hands. Use it and abuse it. It is a fact that few gentlemen have taken the trouble to emerge from the maternal ... that's their weak point; exploit it.

Well anchored in the conviction that the man must be the Man-tra, insist that he be totally, permanently available. Don't be a woman-root but a woman-vine that retains and impedes. Capture the male, absorb him, eat him day after day. Is it in his nature to go outside, move around, travel? Deny him this right. Consider each moment he spends "out" as a betrayal, an outrage, his way of denying you. *The monster!*

According to the extent he deceives you since he's nothing but a man, strip yourself of the grace and aptitudes of the woman to transform yourself into a shrew. No longer be a companion but the embodiment of blame – a bitter, unfounded exigency. Start from a principle which will allow the rest to follow: *Man, your man, is not enough.* Not enough what? It doesn't matter. You don't need to know exactly.

Not masculine enough, feminine enough, present enough, discrete enough, busy enough, available enough. *Not being "enough," at the same time, he's "too."* Too absent, too present, too sensitive, too insensitive, too strong, too weak and so forth.

Stop saying a word to him unless it's a word of bitter and massive reproach. Become, for he who shares your life, the very image of reproach; the incarnation of deaf, constant, and sulky reprobation. He must feel vaguely guilty each time you appear, just like he did each time his mother glanced his way.

Develop the habit – it's easy, don't worry – to only speak to him in a bitter tone somewhere between the shriek, the swallowed sob and the hoarse bark. Let everything in your physical attitude, your facial expressions, the way you are when he's around, drive home the message: you're not up to it, you're not the Other, you're not the Man-tra. Like a skunk releasing its fetid fluid, emanate dissatisfaction, effuse bitterness.

Ask him for everything and its opposite, *the important thing being to make it impossible for him to succeed even before he undertakes anything, whatever it is and whatever he does.* The key word is "impotence." It's essentially a matter of rendering him inoperative, good for nothing, null and void, but without, for all that, making him disappear. He must stay there, never escape you, as if eternally present – in the maternal word, time is abolished – but the presence must be useless, an inept yet indispensable element that allows your matriarchy to roll on smoothly.

To render him impotent, make him feel, day after day, that he *cannot*. Cannot what? Satisfy you, of course. Every day, face him with an impossibility. For example, demand he be a socially affirmed man, a good financial provider who makes a good public appearance, while insisting he be very available, doesn't travel, has the time, lots of time, ever so much time ...

Little does it matter what your exigencies are provided they are numerous, constant and contradictory. If his job doesn't keep him very busy and he's home a lot, reproach him for hanging around the house too much. If he's very involved in his activities, complain about the fact that he's "never there." Loudly demand he be available weekends, vacations, evenings out, for dinners and, when he complies, do your utmost – and there's lots you can do – to inspire the desire in him to be elsewhere and not to try again for a long time. Headaches, your period, various indispositions, bad (very bad) moods ... you possess an entire arsenal of clever methods to make him fail. When he's too busy, be in great form. Always out of synch, never in adhesion. Don't accept what he gives you when he gives it to you and whine that he gives you nothing when that's the case.

Along these lines it will be to your advantage to *ruminate* about the past. Be more bitchy than any wounded bitch in that mournful whimpering about what wasn't but should have been. Use the time you spend together to deplore the moments spent apart. Go on the principle that you can't enjoy the present because of some past that was not what it should have been. *The past proves extremely convenient in that it can't be changed but only ruminated, endlessly gone over.*

From the point of view of the path, there again ask the impossible from him: expect that he be a "great disciple" – and, why not, a spiritual master – and recognized as such, but only on the condition that you come first; his priority, his true master, his direction and landmark must, in fact, be you – the other one, the Spiritual Friend, only being a flattering but inoperative reference as soon as things get serious, that's to say, as soon as you tend to the perverse business of staging the Kouple drama.

Since long conflicts are always fuelled by good, old, deep-rooted hate, it will be advantageous to feed the Kouple battle on the war of the sexes. Ladies, isn't man's greatest fault the fact that he's a man? From the start, haven't you had the impression, vague but recurrent, that something's missing and that the other, the male, the enemy, seems to have an unfair advantage? Continue along this line and dig it deeply by playing on his confusion: *if you're not completely a woman, that's because he's not a Man-tra, and if he's not a Man-tra, he's not really a man.*

My Om is You

Gentlemen, on your part you have at your disposal, in response to this terrorism, two reactions apparently contradictory but equally effective in that they perpetuate the conflict and prohibit the passage of Kouple to couple.

You can go along, even run with the Womb-man's game, attempting at all costs to be that famous Man-tra, a desperate attempt that's doubly efficient: seeking to make yourself Man-tra, you prevent yourself from maturing into a man; not becoming man, you maintain your partner in her condition as the Womb-man, making access to the status of woman difficult. This is, in effect, one of the Spiritual Enemy's great talents – to present, like a mirror, inversed truths. If one is to believe the gospel according to the mind, Womb-man isn't woman because man isn't Man-tra; whereas, of course, but – that should go unspoken – Womb-man will only become woman if Man-tra evolves into man … *Enter, then, in the infernal round of the maternal, engulf yourself in the fissure.* Hurrying after the other in this fissure is always an excellent idea from the viewpoint of mental and spiritual sabotage. The good little boy, endlessly and exhaustively seeking to satisfy the demands of the Womb-man, to fulfil her needs, to make Mommy happy. Feel guilty, useless, inadequate. You'll thus grow weary of life until you're sickened by it and sink into a mournful misogyny. Women, faced with the man thus emasculated, you will enjoy the legitimization of your discontent. How convenient it is that he's a wretch, a wimp, just good enough to roll out pie dough because he justifies your persisting in *gnawing on that old bone of your dissatisfaction.*

Generally speaking, *never leave your mind with its mouth empty, without a bone to gnaw.* Everything is going pretty well, existence proves to be tolerable, your companion isn't, when all is said and done, such a bad guy? Watch out, you could get the crazy idea to take advantage of this in order to turn toward the essential, to get further into your practice of the path on a daily basis while innocently enjoying what life offers you. Negativity tolerates no letdown. If there's no obvious reason for seeing life as gray, invent one. That homemade fabrication of misery will be no problem. It suffices that the ideal remain your norm and definition of reality. Gnaw the bone, again and again; hang on for dear life to that old, bloody meat made of your grievances, unfulfilled expectations and repressed bitterness.

Men, if you don't flatten yourself, or when the posture called "doormat" begins to irritate you, why not flip over to the pseudo-virile reaction? Feel free to strike out, hurt, humiliate emotionally and, why not, physically, physical violence being the last resort of the impotent man who at least retains the superiority of his muscular mass. Punch, grotesquely pound your fist on the table, have authority flashes, attacks of masculinity which will only make your partner snicker derisively. Physically you can bend the woman; but you'll never be stronger than her scorn.

Following this logic, you can always indulge in vaudeville, an updated version, of course, more sophisticated, and cheat on your companion. The exciting thing about adultery is that, as it restores your virility at very low cost, it quickly allows you to tremble before two women rather than one. It also makes it possible *to avoid two relationships at one time* – while at the same time giving the impression of living one of them intensely while you endure the other. Thus you ensconce yourself in flight while madam has complete latitude to drape herself in the dignity of the outraged wife. The woman scorned remains one of the great, tragic roles of the Kouple, the role of the macho-bastard being no less grandiose in its mediocrity.

Wretch or bastard then, but above all never a man capable of nourishing the feminine in setting, when necessary, the limits that inspire love. *Harpy or subjugated, but above all never a woman* capable of giving the man roots so that he can rise and become dignified.

Among the Members of Hellish Family, I Want the Child

And if the above-mentioned strategies are not enough to break up the couple or transform it into an infernal machine good for sundering the union, there remains a trump card, usually played by the woman but which, as always, demands the complicity of the man to produce its evil effects.

This powerful weapon that your Enemy suggests you use to finish off the relationship has the angelic face of the child. Use of the child for destructive purposes is especially delectable: it not only allows the partners to hurt each other, but under the same impulse to devastate someone innocent.

In using the child as the engine of the Kouple war, you sabotage the present and sow the bad seed of sabotages to come. The child thus turned into an instrument will, in effect, have every chance, when reaching adulthood, of replaying the scenario, becoming in turn a link in the chain of ordinary tragedy.

Women, begin by placing your offspring in the register of the sublime. The IDEAL, nothing but the IDEAL, with capital letters everywhere. The child thus becomes the Child, the Savior, the alpha and omega, your tailor-made redeemer, the divine response to all your dissatisfactions. *He is born, the Divine infant, for the glory of the Womb-man and the salvation of her world.* Let trumpets blow and cymbals crash until the eardrums of your immediate and not so immediate entourage burst. The man, proving not to be the Man-tra, has disappointed you? No problem! From now on it will be the fruit of your womb who inherits the weighty mission of atoning for the sins of the male universe, and thus fulfills you. Place all your hopes in him or her, even before s/he is born.

The ideal would be that at this stage the man – having become that cumbersome third party which one, all things considered, no longer needs – is already out of the picture, eliminated even before the Savior appears. The deviations of our society will be a great help to you. They permit, in effect, and even insidiously encourage the fabrication of the Child by the woman alone, the man having been reduced to the rung of simple sperm donor. This unheard of progress lets us glimpse the realization of an old fantasy that was highly inaccessible until the present: *the final solution at last applied to man as a superfluous and disturbing presence.* Who still needs a father, that out-of-date and bothersome figure? Thus, woman, if you can, fabricate your very own child, make him or her "all by yourself" like a big girl. You can thus form with him or her a remarkable duo, an undeclarable Kouple.

The girl child will be your accomplice in a world having

celebrated the final defeat of the male; the boy, your little man, a male finally at your mercy, devoted body and soul to the maternal cause.

Certain gentlemen will complacently lend themselves to this ideal scenario and disappear right away, too panicked by the perspective of being, perhaps, pushed to grow up. Nevertheless, not all of them will efface themselves so obligingly. There are still a great number of boys who glimpse, if only vaguely, the unprecedented chance to become a man that paternity offers them. If, unluckily, you find yourself encumbered with a male thus pretending, the fop, to accede to the status of father, it will be necessary to use the full range of your resources. There again, never forget that you have, *a priori*, the advantage, the father not being a father unless the mother wishes it so. Thus you need only not wish it so, tranquilly and resolutely.

Therefore, drive your male into a corner and leave him hanging there; the sooner, the better. From the moment the pregnancy is revealed, push him away insidiously. Having supplied the sperm, he's fulfilled his role, accomplished his function as donor. This fleeting moment of glory is over and he can now regain the wings that you will take care to never let him leave.

The teaching at this stage of operation will be useful to you: all the spiritual traditions have indeed exalted the role and the image of the Mother – the very first other; unavoidable foundation of affectivity; and, thus, the determining factor of one's primal relationship to life. You need only pervert these truths. Under the pretext of being a mother, *remember how well the word rhymes with smother and turn yourself into a smothering mother, that invasive entity that stifles all.*

This evolution will be all the more evident to you if you, yourself, had no father or a very unsubstantial one. Let your tentacles close around the child. Plant your talons in his or her flesh and don't let go, ever. Wrap yourself around this little being. *As soon as you're a mother, cease to be a spouse.* You only pretended to be one to serve your ends. The moment has finally come to bring the masquerade to a halt. Send that innocuous male back to his silly little games.

Of course, go on sexual strike: insidiously prolong the inevitable weariness and adaptation of your body that goes along with pregnancy and then giving birth into an instituted state that suffers no discussion. Once again, the sperm having been furnished, the sexual relationship, a place of intimate encounter, becomes superfluous and in the end useless. Make him fully aware of the inappropriate and bestial nature of his vile physical demands. He should feel himself a primate in the face of the sublime encounter of smothering mother-smothered child. What becomes him, as a man, to patiently accept for a time – abstinence – impose on him for an indefinite period of time. But make sure to never clearly state it. Just let it be known that you "won't" for the moment, a moment which, why not, could well extend into forever. Your disaffection as regards sexuality will have the advantage of fuelling his frustration and therefore rage, which will allow you then to denounce loudly and clearly his execrable disposition. The more you maintain that convenient state of affairs, the more you'll push him to seek carnal consolation elsewhere, thus tailor-making him a bastard suit.

Construct an insurmountable wall around the Mother-Child Kouple. If the man persists in trying to take his place as the father, eject him just as persistently. Justify yourself by evoking the necessary and irreplaceable fusion of the beginnings of life; thus instill in your partner, already somewhat disconcerted as all men tend to be when their child is born, the feeling that he's in the way or, more exactly, incongruous and obsolete. Reproach him his slightest attempts to get close to his child, condemn him as the thickheaded brute who just doesn't know a thing. Never consent to leave him alone with his son or daughter – while of course complaining that he doesn't help you enough; that he leaves you all the responsibility; in short, that he's merely taking up space, an object as cumbersome as it is useless. Does he take it upon himself to change and dress the little angel? Whatever he does, he obviously can't do it right. Don't deprive yourself of pointing this out to him so he'll get discouraged as quickly as possible if, by chance, he should have some vague notion about participatory paternity.

Persist along these lines during the time your child is growing up. Don't let the man get too close to the child, and when he attempts to approach him or her, stress the inadequacy of that approach. The games he proposes aren't the right ones; his initiatives are, on principle, ill chosen. Having forced him into a presence-absence, you can advantageously insist, once you've had enough, that from this point on he take charge of everything. He'll of course prove hardly capable of it, thus supplying you with ample grounds for criticism, complaints and recriminations. In sum, *be the abortionist of a birth that was nevertheless planned, that of the father*.

Men, willingly consent to this abortion. To that end, take care to show ever increasing infantilism. A birth is a seism, a serious disturbance in the existence and mode of functioning of the couple. Don't weather the seism, don't stand fast against the shock, *don't be up to it*. Begin by doing your best to live the period of pregnancy and all its commotion badly. Suspiciously regard that ever-rounding belly, the forms mutating in a fashion that's a far cry from the criteria of feminine beauty publicized everywhere, that is to say the fashion model with the anorexic silhouette. Drop her sexually; play on a fear obviously latent in her, if by chance she still feels she's part of a couple, the fear of no longer appealing to you. Once the baby is born, be jealous of the little intruder come to break up the game of mirrors you and your better-half play. You "wished you were dead" when a brother or sister arrived in a family where all the precautions were not taken to protect you from receiving the shock full in the face? No one in your family cared enough to make sure you could assimilate that momentous event and turn it into a maturing factor, undoubtedly a little brutal but, all things considered, positive? That is just perfect; let the wound reopen so that right away you resent the newborn who's come to steal your wife, just as once your mother was stolen from you. Take care not to tolerate the blessed and necessary fusion during the first days of life which will mean, in fact, that for a time your wife is less available sexually and emotionally. If she's not determined to be a smothering mother, try to turn her into one through spite. With your infantilism, your little-boy recriminations, your tantrums and sulks, give her every reason to resent you until all she feels is scorn. Sexuality remains an irreplaceable measure of your emotional condition. A man-child doesn't accept a momentary privation of "cuddling." Be that man-child, pathetic in his inopportune need. Feel you've been rejected, pushed aside, excluded, no matter what your companion tries. This is the moment to begin one or several affairs, to beg elsewhere the tender kisses that Mommy hasn't, for the moment, got the time to give you.

Just when it's expected that you take your place as a father, sneak away. Do not take upon yourself the solitude of he who is expected to dispense the law. Don't tolerate any loss of affection. This way, you'll find yourself more and more discredited and your couple will pay the price, seeing as it's true that mutual respect is the armor of a durable relationship.

The Kamikaze Kouple

In the preceding pages your Enemy suggested the one-thousand-and-one strategies of flight and avoidance of the relationship as a testing ground of transformation.

There is still one more – a marvel of duplicity – which consists of *remaining*, against all logic, even though the couple, stuck in the delirium of the Kouple, not only has ceased to help you mature but has begun *to erode your life's energy.*

Thanks to the Devil, your devoted servant, there are "households" that transform themselves into miniature extermination camps in which no one, man, woman, child, or even friend or relation, is spared. The entire field of existence is contaminated, the social and professional domains poisoned by the toxic fumes a relationship grown destructive gives off.

If as your Adversary hopes, you're thus caught up in the spiral of a dying intimacy, use the teaching to deny the evidence and not to perceive the moment when the only issue for preserving mental, physical and spiritual life is to bring the relationship to an end. As always, and according to a process explained in a chapter of this treatise, it's a matter of making use of words and considerations, in themselves precious and true, and pretending to apply them when and where they don't or no longer apply. In the name of the path, the master, the dharma, the Church, the Ideal, faithfulness, commitment and other lofty values, persist in destroying yourself. You'll thus be an accomplice in the destruction of the other, or should we say the others – since you can make your children bear the burden of a union maintained against all healthy common sense and survival instinct. Take care not to see the line of demarcation between persistence in the face of obstacles and blind obstinacy; forget a basic truth: in order to work, progress from the Kouple fantasy to the reality of the couple; in order to build a life together it's necessary that together you should want that life. One person alone is unable to shoulder the edifice of the relationship especially if his or her partner, possessed by the Enemy, is at the same time trying to dismantle it. You have the sentiment, in all honesty, of having run out of options and you begin to note the futility of your efforts? Even your vital force is showing signs of weakening? Pay no attention, continue; repeat to yourself that a disciple, a father, a mother, a Christian, a man or a woman engaged in the path doesn't ever divorce, doesn't seek a separation. *Cover your appetite for life with an ever thicker layer of the ideal.*

Stay, at the cost of your life, even if it will perhaps take some time for you to actually die, to quit that body that's become a prison with no prospects for evolution and liberty.

Women, your husband mocks you, avoids all his responsibilities? Maybe he drinks, takes drugs, abuses mentally and physically? You should stay, he's your guru, the opportunity for martyrdom that will sanctify you, the instrument of your salvation. Men, your wife wounds your dignity day after day, attacks your masculine integrity, refuses herself to you, denies you your right to a life as a husband and father, and only stays at your side to emit endless complaints? Remain with her, tolerate everything, *confound acceptance of what is in the moment with the infantile inability to say "no" whenever necessary*. Rationalize the neurotic dynamic, through which you mire yourself in a relationship that's become a swamp, with the wise words of the sages and pious sayings. The essential thing always and forever is that you founder, that the objectives pursued by the Enemy with your collaboration – that's to say your human and spiritual drowning – be magnificently accomplished thanks to the perversion of that very path which lured you with promises of unconditional peace and lasting joy.

Let the couple, that territory of intimate openness, become a bunker within whose walls are perpetuated the values of an imaginary entity that's grown decadent.

5

Emotion Is Always Justified

How to Get Carried Away
and Stay There

There is but one God, Emotion, and expression is his prophet.

- The Spiritual Enemy

A ll spiritual traditions have insisted on the necessity of "purging the passions," the indispensable "purification of the affects," the need to "ride the tiger" ... in short, on mastering the energy called "emotion."

In fact, we can't imagine a "saint" or "sage" being a slave to anger, dominated by fear, possessed of unbridled ambition, carried away by an excess of violence, crushed under the weight of sadness, nurturing spite and bitterness, no longer feeling joy, or simply subject to all the aggravations, jealousies, depressions and provocations that are the common mortal's lot.

Hollower than Thou

Yet, whereas all teachings and teachers have abundantly dwelt on emotion, your Enemy rejoices to note the extent to which emotion – of course adorned with the masks of charity, tenderness, devotion, and all the good intentions that pave the road to hell – reigns equally, if not more absolutely, at the core of ashrams, monasteries, churches, spiritual centers and other associations dedicated to cultivating the essential.

What disputes, what pettiness, intrigues, divisions, what violence, manipulations, falling outs, exclusions, power struggles, in short, what emotions there are in the spawning ground of these supposedly "holy" places – not only within the notorious "cults," but even in the most respectable and respected places.

Every spiritual seeker determined to never find will thus be well advised to learn the lessons of this omnipresence. The goal is limpid: *whatever the nobility and sincerity of your aspirations, whatever the profoundness or your metaphysical intuitions and the quality of your mystical experiences, it's important that they always find themselves savagely attacked by the too human reality of your emotional condition.*

Emotional? Me? Never!

The surest way to strengthen the hold of an adverse force is to deny its existence. Consequently, *begin by not according the slightest place, on the path, to your emotions and to any kind of work which would allow you to relate to them in a more conscious way.* If your Enemy – at other times called the devil or the evil spirit until people decided, most opportunely, and under his influence, that he didn't exist – maintains his hold on this planet, it is largely thanks to the lack of understanding or the underestimation of the role of childish emotions everywhere: in the heart of the couple, the family, the educational system, at all levels of the social and political pyramid, and on into the highest spheres. Emotion is a dictator hidden in the shadows who secretly pulls the strings of the world. This is a supposedly well-kept secret that everyone in fact knows without ever admitting it. We all act as if emotion was not reigning as an absolute monarch from the beginning to the end of our life.

Isn't it amusing to note one simple fact: in spite of the discovery – or rediscovery – by a dangerous genius named Freud, of the unconscious and its processes, one continues in large measure to act as if human beings were, above all, rational creatures whose acts and decisions proceeded from reason rather than emotion; as if it wasn't demands, fears, impulses and representations crystallized in early childhood that governed bodies and intellects having reached so called adulthood …

This *conspiracy of silence about the domination of childishness* marvelously confuses the issues and greatly facilitates the Enemy's job. The fact that, having done no real work in order to emerge from their psychological prison, most men and women don't know themselves and are still children is universally and consistently denied. Prince of lies, the evil spirit maintains the most pernicious of humbugs: human beings are adults and not, just under the surface, scared, manipulating children animated by a desperate need to be recognized and, given this fact, unfit to truly take the other into consideration.

Consequently, faithful to your intention to participate, through your little lies, in the reign of the Great Lie, *deny*, a priori, *the all powerfulness of emotion, first and foremost, in yourself*. Carried away by emotional blindness? Me? Never, or so very rarely … Let if be clearly understood that it's not emotion that dictates your political choices, motivates your professional orientation, directs your family life.

In any case, let it be very clear that your childish emotions have absolutely nothing to do with your spiritual search. It's vital that any eventuality of emotion interfering in your perception of the path be the object of fierce denial. *Start with the principle that you essentially are an adult, free of Mommy and Daddy*. Thus, you'll be at leisure to place the "liberation" exalted by all spiritual paths, far, far into the lofty spheres of the metaphysical, out of reach of the psychological swamp.

Don't forget a fundamental principle of the Enemy's strategy: *always rely on a truth to fuel a lie*. Thus, start with an incontestable given: the spiritual dimension has absolutely nothing to do with the psychological dimension. Reinforced by this axiom, act as if the psychology of each person did not determine, if not entirely, at least to a great extent, the manner in which the spiritual quest will be approached, understood, lived.

There are some psychoanalysts, the unknowing zealous servants of the Enemy, who insist on relegating all spiritual aspirations to the realm of maladies that should be cured: infantile projections, search for the father, nostalgia for the maternal fusion, fantasies of absolute power … According to them, religious thirst and spiritual aspirations are mere neuroses. Adopt the exactly opposite point of view: consider all forms of work on the unconscious as, if not charlatanism, at least an unhealthy exploration of interior demons, which it would be wiser to leave sleeping. Backing yourself up with the remarkable works of the great esoteric writer René Guénon, you can even consider psychoanalysis and its derivatives as satanic inventions, symptoms of the decline of the Western world.

In short, it's a matter of *refusing, in the name of spirituality, any consideration of the psychological dimension.* Never mind that unconscious forces, although under other names, have always been approached and taken seriously by the spiritual traditions. Expressed though the form of symbols and images, the shadow was and still is the subject of work that relies on tools such as intensively practiced meditation, visualization, and other techniques and approaches. You will also most opportunely overlook the fact that close, continuous relationship with a spiritual master worthy of the name is no stranger – and that's a euphemism – to the process of "transference" so essential to the relationship of analyzed and analyst.

To sum things up, *be, to the great glory of "spirituality," ignorant of and indifferent to the psychological dimension of the human being; better yet, implacably oppose the spiritual and the psychological. Declare yourself, on principle, hostile to all forms of purification of the unconscious.*

Liberation cannot have anything to do with being free from Mommy and Daddy, and you've got to passionately denounce whoever entertains such notions. The path is about liberating oneself from "illusion," "ignorance," "*maya*," which of course have nothing to do with your illusions, your ignorance and your blindness to whatever plots are hatching in you. If you take the risk to concede that it's necessary to free oneself from psychology, be certain that this means psychology *in general* and not your psychology *in particular*.

However, the worst needing to be envisioned, what avoidance strategy should be adopted if the teaching you pretend to follow forces you, despite all your bad faith, to recognize the existence of the unconscious and the necessity to purify it as you advance on the path?

Down with Psychology, Up with Spirituality

Here again, it suffices to take a truth and twist it into a lie. You'll base this on two facts: 1) the unconscious forces have been taken into account in the most ancient ascetic disciplines; 2) if the world and society have greatly changed since the era of

Buddha, Dogen, Shankaracharya or Saint Benedict the human being remains essentially identical, endowed with the same possibilities and subject to the same stumbling blocks.

From that point, and relying heavily on these statements, consider that the path – such as it has reached you in its strictly traditional form – is in itself sufficient, and is perfectly adapted to you in your actual condition. Don't doubt that the means likely to prove efficient with the adepts born and raised in societies completely different from ours show themselves to be equally operative for the average, contemporary Westerner interested in spirituality. Don't imagine there could be a difference between mature disciples, psychologically well-balanced individuals animated by an intense aspiration within a culture centered around spiritual values, and sincere amateurs, emotionally crippled men and women prey to a multitude of contradictory desires, ensconced in a naïve arrogance, products of a society that's democratic, certainly, but obsessed with profit and comfort. Affirm that zazen alone, yoga postures alone, prayer alone will suffice to carry out the necessary psychological purification. Don't take into consideration that, if the human being has not, in fact, essentially changed, he nonetheless approaches the spiritual teachings in an entirely different spiritual condition and an altogether different context than the seekers of yore. Conveniently overlook the fact that spiritual masters as eminent as Swami Prajnanpad and, in the West, Karlfried Graf Dürckheim, recognized, in the first half of the twentieth century, the necessity to put modern tools – psychology, analysis, therapy – at the service of the ancient ways proposed to today's men and women.

Along this line, it will always be an advantage to refer to the example of the greatest in order to apply their own criteria to yourself. Affirm, and rightly so, that Milarepa, Shankara, Buddha, Rumi, Kangyur Rinpoche, Teresa of Avila, Francis of Assisi, Ramana Maharshi, Ramdas, Chandra Swami, the Dalai Lama and others in the same category never underwent any kind of therapy or analysis; then conclude, less rightly so, that you can therefore, *a priori*, do without it too. (See Appendix A for brief information about these spiritual giants.) Read Irina Tweedie's *Chasm of Fire* and the autobiography of Amritanandamayi, then act as if it's obvious that what was true for them is true for you. Apply to yourself the criteria of giants, forgetting you are but a dwarf in that respect. Did Irina Tweedie leave everything to be available day and night to her Sufi master while you spend at most a few weeks – when it's not a few days –a year with a master or instructor who suggests a few practices that you are entirely at liberty to follow or not? That's only a detail. Were those great Tibetan masters you admire so much, for the most part, trained since childhood in strict methods and in a context that no longer exists? See that as merely an anecdote. Let it be a given that your surface sincerity – which you find immeasurably deep – will clearly do; that your lukewarm commitment – burning intensity, according to your mind – will consume the obstacles; that your occasional investment – total and unreserved, you will of course protest – entitles you to reach the heights of mysticism in no time. In short, *you'll give little but will receive a lot.* You need barely scratch at the door and it will open to you. You will be utterly transformed without having been intimately shaken. You will pass through the walls of your psychological prison without shifting the smallest stone. Radical conversion, metanoia, "enlightenment," that famous "awakening" everyone brags about will be yours at low cost simply because you will have deigned to be interested in it and have invested a little of your time, money, and energy in it. The ego is such that it dreams of filling its belly without paying the bill, of enjoying power without tolerating the obligations that go with it, of gaining millions without working or paying taxes. Spirituality, a domain after all vague and intangible if one doesn't approach it with the necessary rigor, furnishes the ego inexhaustible material for compensatory dreams. No one in his right mind will entertain hopes of becoming a concert pianist without seeing the necessity of devoting one's life to music, with hours and hours of daily practice as the key; however, it is so easy to let one's mind dwell in fantasies of "liberation" without, in the least, taking into consideration the price of that freedom.

Let it be understood, then: meditation, practiced a half hour daily and sometimes complemented by a few intensive sessions when you're feeling zealous, will conquer your neurosis; it's sufficient that Amritanandamayi takes you in her arms once or twice a year – certainly you'll have to wait in line a few hours, but that's not asking a lot when you're motivated – for you to be completely clear in your relationship to your mother. Simply through the power of his benediction, Chandra Swami will turn you into an ardent god-intoxicated soul. Taking refuge with a Tibetan lama, topped off with a few quick retreats which include the recitation of mantras and the visualization of tantric divinities, will cure you of your infantilism; one or two annual, week-long retreats at Arnaud Desjardins' ashram, stays during which your practice will consist of thinking about it from time to time, will transform you into a great disciple capable of looking down on all work on the unconscious and of approaching the shores of the highest metaphysical levels right away.

Though naïve, ignorant and arrogant, this attitude offers some splendid results in terms of anti-wisdom and the perversion of a spiritual ideal: religious communities populated by neurotics who are rationalizing and justifying their problems by mystical or theological concepts; ashrams infested with great meditators who can't stop talking about pure consciousness but who are jealous and petty as soon as they come out of their meditation; devotional paths whose adepts regress to the state of little children ferociously vying for the attention of the Mommy-Daddy-Master; strict adepts of vedanta proclaiming that "there is no one" but around whom, nevertheless, there certainly seems to be "someone" as soon as you contradict them or life mistreats them; a frightening proportion of pedophile priests protected by an ecclesiastical institution disarmed when facing a backlash of repression; humanitarian associations led by the power hungry; charitable organizations managed by the money hungry; surly militants of non-violence; and other vindictive apostles of peace. The results, indeed, speak for themselves.

The Superego Path to Becoming Inhuman

What should you do, nevertheless, if, in the teaching you pretend to follow, there inopportunely arises the question of "emotions" and the necessity to free oneself from them? Remember that you risk nothing as long as all of this remains vague. The mind, rest assured, makes its bed in a haze. Fortified by this law, cultivate approximation as concerns the very concept of emotion along the path. There again, rely on a truth to cultivate a lie: justify your lack of rigor by arguing that the way cannot remain on a purely intellectual level, that it is, first and foremost, a matter of "heart," of "feeling," and other notions which will remain incredibly vague as long as they are envisioned from an emotional context which precisely prohibits access to authentic sentiment.

Therefore, be as vague as possible about what is meant, on the path, by "emotion": make no distinction between emotion (that which moves you outside of yourself, carries you away, puts you "beside yourself," as the current expressions so well put it), and sentiment or feeling (that intelligence of the heart which brings you back to yourself and allows you to experience, to feel deeply, rather than reacting on the surface).

As far as feeling anything is concerned, let your only experience be that of emotion – blind, excessive and stupid. Don't envision differentiating it in any way from sentiment: lucid, sober and, at the same time, vibrant.

This carefully maintained lack of distinction about everything that concerns the heart will allow you to brandish a very convenient objection to refute the necessity of working toward affective purification: but, don't you see, emotion is life! One should not, after all, under the pretext of liberating oneself from emotions, become a robot that no longer feels anything! *To better guarantee your failure along the path, you will profit from forging yourself a vague and, in the end, unenviable concept of the very goal of the path.* Following this logic, the path is about "no longer having emotions"; becoming a cold monster unable to feel anything; "saying yes" to all and everything, denying oneself the possibility to take a position or act in an attempt to make things evolve in the desired direction. In short, *consider the ascetic discipline not as the divine path to becoming human, but as the superego's path to becoming inhuman.* You'll thus discreetly succeed in turning the path into a dead end: what a marvelous impasse it is, that which consists of pretending to follow a path whose goal appears not only inaccessible but, in any case, utterly undesirable. What sensible person would want, in effect, "to say yes to everything" and "no longer have emotions"?

In order to maintain the obscurity, cultivate approximation as to what "being carried away by emotion" precisely means. You will understand even less what it is to be "emotional" – in the specific sense given this term on the path – if you have no idea of what it would be not to be carried away. Therefore, do your best to always remain carried away, away from yourself, uprooted from the axis of presence – and to never be rooted, restored to yourself, in the integrity of vigilance, not carried away by thoughts and the emotions produced by thoughts. In this way you won't even conceive of the existence within you of an "I" that could be altogether different from "me." Not "you" as a self-obsessed individual but you as a person, "you, yourself, in your own intrinsic dignity" – to use a formula of the pernicious Swami Prajnanpad.

The "neutrality" advocated not only by that Swami but, under diverse names, by all spiritual teachings, will remain unknown to you and you will thus be stripped of all landmarks in your approach of any practice relating to the emotional level, like a prisoner pretending to escape without having the slightest reference of what freedom is about. The very word "neutral" will only evoke an insipid condition, in itself contrary to life. From that point you'll consider yourself carried away by emotion only when you actually are furious, desperate, excited, anxious, feverish; you won't have the slightest consciousness that you are indeed carried away from the instant that you are not "neutral"; put otherwise, that you are practically never free of the hold of emotion in its insidious form, at the latent state.

Completely miss a simple truth: the natural state is peace, fundamental tranquillity, even though agitation can rise to the surface. *Don't glimpse the fact that emotion exists from the moment you are not completely at peace here and now.* Conceive emotion only as a great disturbance and not as a slight uneasiness. Ignoring the interior positioning that keeps you in balance, don't imagine that you can be technically "unbalanced" as soon as you deviate, even a little, from your center of gravity.

Envisioning only so called "negative" emotions without taking into consideration outbursts of "happy" emotions will further fuel this precious confusion. Don't suspect that "liberating oneself from suffering" – emotional suffering, of course – implies to be liberated from "happiness" as well.

This misconception about the very nature of emotions will lead you to believe that most of the time you really do live in the world such as it is, never suspecting that you are, in fact, only in contact with your world, entirely subjective, secreted by your fears, desires, conditioning and prejudices. *Don't see your thoughts as quotations*, the unconscious appropriation of this or that ambient discourse, but as the articulation of a lucid thought; don't see your emotions as imitations, replicas of reactions that, as a child, you picked up from "the adults," but as the free and legitimate expression of rational vision; *as to your actions, don't see them as caricatures*, the gesticulations imposed by thoughts and emotions, but as gestures performed by a lucid person, conscious of the reasons for his acts and of their eventual consequences.

Therefore, imagining yourself to be a free individual, as such capable of choosing rather than simply being a machine which reacts according to the whims of stimuli brought on by existence, you will expect others, also seen as "free and responsible," to make "the right choice," that is to say, yours. This will allow you to divide humanity into two definite categories: the "good" – those who see the world as you do – and the "bad" – assholes ... those who don't see it at all the way you do ... poor senseless morons incapable of converting themselves to the metric system of truth, a system emitted by you and tailored to your measure.

In regard to "the drunkenness of emotional intoxications" (Swami Prajnanpad) *you will adopt the position of the addict denying his addiction*: me, hooked? Not at all! I am in control of my drug-use and, moreover, I can stop whenever I want. You will not measure the extent of your enslavement to thoughts and emotions. Not considering yourself a slave, you will have no reason to aspire being emancipated. At most, you'll want to bring a few improvements to your life in that prison which, viscerally, you don't sense as being one.

How to Be Carried Away and Remain So

What can one do, however, if emotion is there, flagrant, undeniable, as conspicuous as an elephant in your interior landscape? How do you avoid working on emotions if you can no longer pretend not to be carried away? Always at your service, your Enemy suggests a strategy that is as perverse as it is efficient: *recognize in you the existence of emotion, but consider it, each time, as perfectly justified*. "Yes, okay, I'm enraged, but you can't be expected to accept everything, can you? ... Of course I am screaming, eyes bugging out, at my two-year-old son, but it's because he's impossible and you can't let him always do as he pleases! ... Yes, I'm having an anxiety attack over the possibility of germ warfare or a nuclear reactor being blown up, but you've got to admit there's good reason to be afraid!"

Along this line, it's not only imperative to maintain that emotion is justified and necessary, but also to become indignant at the very idea that one could do without emotion: "What? This client not only refuses to pay his bill but sends me a letter full of insults and you don't understand why I'm beside myself? ... Well then, you've got to live in indifference and not react to the world events that are as disquieting as they are tragic! ... What! You think I could feel something else than utter despair when I've just been diagnosed with a serious disease!"

It's understood that this positioning always relies on the confusion between emotion and feeling, whose importance your Enemy has already stressed. As long as emotion is not technically differentiated from feeling or sentiment, the perspective of "no longer having emotions" is terrifying because it proposes, in fact, a robotic condition characterized by pathological indifference. Undistinguished from sentiment, emotion is still seen as fuel necessary to life itself, a vital energy, indispensable for feeling the positive or negative impacts of existence and for coping with situations.

Well-established in this confusion, don't envision, for an instant, the spiritual perspective according to which "emotion is never justified" (Swami Prajnanpad).

From the start, don't bother trying to understand what that formula really means. Don't take the adjective "justified" to mean "adjusted" to the situation – in the same way that an expense proves to be justified or not; in other words "necessary," taking into account what is. Rather understand this term as referring to a run-of-the-mill moral according to which it would be unseemly, or plain "bad," to be experiencing emotions. *Translate "emotion is never justified" into "I don't have the right to have emotions," "I should not be feeling what I am feeling right now."* This negative approach will be all the easier for you if you've been impregnated by a perverted Christianity in which what was simply an error in orientation in view of the goal pursued becomes a "sin"; that is to say, a fault that deserves punishment, the proof of the intrinsically evil nature of the human being/sinner who, moreover, should be ashamed. Being so tricky, mind is expert at transforming everything that it encounters. Mind knows how to recycle Buddhism, vedanta, or any other teaching into a Christianizing system founded on interior division and guilt. Having a long time ago succeeded in perverting the message of Christ, it is child's play for the mind to twist the most liberating truths into a guilt-making tangle.

Thus persuaded that emotion is an evil, a fault, a sin, choose to repress everything. Hold back, inhibit, strongly justifying yourself with spiritual formulas. *Let your yes be a no that dares not admit it, let your acceptance be resignation, your letting go a flight, your kindness the fear of rejection.* Automatically stick a "gotta say yes" label on every "no" that crops up, whitewash your aggressiveness with a coating of artificial peace. Season your most ordinary impulses with a sauce of the mystical-spiritual ideal.

"What can a kingdom divided against itself do?" the Galilean asked. Interior division being a guarantee of failure on the path, as it is in existence, be sure to reproach yourself for "having emotions." You must, in the name of the path and on the pretext that "emotion is never justified," resent yourself for feeling what you feel. In short, *incessantly ask yourself to be other than you are in the moment.* This will come very naturally to you if, as is highly likely, you were one of those children to whom parents and teachers kept sending the message: "You are not." Not what? What you should be. Not good, not nice, not gifted, not generous, not hard working, etc. The adjective hardly matters as long as it's preceded by "not." Of course the same message can be transmitted affirmatively: "You're selfish" – which implies: "You shouldn't be. What you are here and now, selfish, is unseemly. In order to be loved, you need to be otherwise – unselfish, generous, sharing your toys with your sister without a fuss, etc." Not being what you should be, you don't deserve to be loved. Thus there you are, condemned to the absurd, to the rage and despair that are the lot of your kind, which is as much to say condemned to emotional death.

Therefore you need only recycle the formulas of the path as parental injunctions; the master, the instructor, God becoming grandiose extensions of Mommy and Daddy in order to continue, in all ill-will, to cut yourself in two and then not to allow yourself to progress along your path. The cause is understood: it's in your very own being that the fault lies. As a child you were not what you should have been. In other words, you didn't succeed in rendering yourself worthy of your parents' love; having thus lamentably failed, not having been loved because you weren't loveable, you are today (like yesterday) that worthless person, fundamentally incapable of being the disciple you must nevertheless be in order to receive the love of the master, God, life.

Who or What it is necessary to be, you are not and cannot be. Your case is hopeless. The proof being that, according to the path, it's necessary to "no longer have emotions," "say yes," "stop reacting," while you, worthless creature, are stuffed with emotions, refusing and reacting. Be ruthless toward yourself, devoid of any benevolence. Mercilessly judge and condemn your feelings. Are you angry? That's horrible. Jealous? How petty … Afraid? What a coward – and anyway didn't Swami Prajnanpad say: "The Way is not for the coward " … Sad? How childish! Aggressive? That's not very nice …

To condemn the emotions arising in you it's important that you appropriate them, that you take them completely personally, consider them yours and yours alone. *My* jealousy, *my* violence, *my* negativity …

Assimilate your emotions to what you are: "I am jealous, violent," and not: "Look at the jealousy, the violence, that arises in me." Rather than seeing them as emotional nuances present in the universe and, as such, susceptible to momentarily taking hold of you, given the appropriate trigger, consider these "passions" as the expression of what you intrinsically are.

Little does it matter that nothing resembles an aggravated driver like another aggravated driver, that there's nothing very original in the jealousy a big brother feels toward his little sister or that a man in love is tormented when his girlfriend looks at another man.

You are aggravated, *you* are jealous, that's *your* "problem," an infirmity that singles *you* out and from which *you* should be exempt. Appropriating negative emotions will quite naturally lead you to also appropriate the positive emotions: *my* very own kindness, *my* generosity, *my* compassion, etc. In short, *everything is personal.* You're having emotions? That's your fault, you shouldn't be having them. As long as you have them, you won't progress. Therefore, reproach yourself for having them and then pretend to be benevolent toward yourself. Yes, I'm a dud, intrinsically bad, crammed with unworthy emotions and undignified thoughts, but I must now show goodwill toward the pathetic individual that I am …

Barricade yourself behind the ego with repeated denials, then ask the ego – which, only understanding the logic of "for" or "against," of winner or loser, ignores goodwill – to show itself "benevolent." In seeking that famous goodwill where it certainly isn't, you'll be sure never to find it.

Above all, consider that your task as a disciple consists of preventing the ego and the mind from doing their work. Since truthfully it's not in your power to prevent them from doing whatever they have to do, but merely to collaborate less and less with them, you'll choose the wrong objective and exhaust yourself at a vain task. Do not practice *with*, always practice *against*.

The goal according to the Spiritual Enemy is not *to be one with*, but *one without*, not to seek unconditional peace, but to bring together, always and everywhere, the conditions necessary to your peace. Therefore you must first be *against* whatever is, in order to eliminate that which *shouldn't be* and forbids you this peace.

Besides maintaining you in a dead end, practice *against* promotes the fermentation within you of emotional energy that results in all sorts of bitterness, psychosomatic illnesses, fabrication of "bile," and more or less serious disorders.

Thus, maintaining a misinterpretation of the formula, "emotion is never justified," will guarantee that you never glimpse its real meaning and the possible practice starting from that understanding.

Never should you envision the simple, practical uselessness of emotion; the fact, not only that it's not necessary, but that it even proves harmful as far as responding to a given situation is concerned.

Don't conceive it possible to go through a difficult or even tragic situation without the intervention of emotion or – at least while one is still progressing along the path – without maintaining and fuelling it. Don't see the extent to which the very fact of being emotionally carried away blinds you and, in prohibiting you from seeing things as they are, leads you down the dead end street of dramatization (positive or negative exaggeration) of reaction, whose consequences you'll later have to assume; in short, of confusion. Certainly you can consider emotion as unpleasant, at least when it is painful, and thus hope to get rid of it on the condition that you don't actually question its justification. That will prevent you from experiencing how much the heart's intelligence reveals itself and inspires the appropriate response when emotion ceases to encumber your affects and gives way to sentiment.

Having no experience of the real benefits of practice, you won't practice and the mind will be safe. *Once well established into emotion considered as inevitable and justified, take care to mire yourself in it.* To accomplish this, you dispose of a recipe made easier because it naturally imposes itself on you: *act under the impulse of emotion.* Nothing is simpler, everything pushes you in that direction! You need only let yourself be carried away by the current of "mechanicality." Born of denial, of the gap between what should be and what is, of the conflict between an ideal you have every intention of hanging onto and reality, emotion as energy first manifests itself as tension. Yet it is in the very nature of all tension to seek release, a release achieved by the unfoldment of the energy, hence through expression. Just as you can't talk sense to a desperately hungry man, emotion desires to express itself and desires this blindly, at whatever cost. Knowing no other law but that of its need, emotion imperiously demands to propagate itself right away, whatever the context and the possible consequences. As such, you need only follow this movement without seeing any further than the end of your agitation. Do not in the least take circumstances into account, do not in any manner try to come back to yourself and consciously get in touch with emotion. Pronounce the hurtful word that burns your lips; don't pause, let alone think, before you speak. Scream your anger, spit out that insult, give that slap, pound the steering wheel in your rage.

There again your non-practice will be based on an adroitly maintained confusion. *Just as you mistake emotion for feeling, mistake reaction for action.*

Action? Your hardly know what that is. It can be defined as the interior and/or exterior response to a given situation by a conscious subject who's in contact with *the* world rather than *his* world, connected to the intelligence of life, fully aware of his acts and their possible consequences. According to Mr Gurdjieff, "Only he that can not do deserves to be called a doer, knows what it is to actually do." Action proceeds from real responsibility, an ability to respond to what existence demands in the moment. Each instant being unique, any action will be unique as well, stemming from a perception of the whole of the data present here and now. Reaction, on the contrary, is something with which you're familiar. Constantly mistaken for action, it is your daily bread. Like the alarm that goes off at the approach of the homeowner as well as the burglar when it's on, reaction goes off whether it's appropriate or not. If action proceeds from a conscious subject exercising his freedom in the moment, reaction just happens in the absence of any subject. It's an automatic motion predetermined by a set of causes that produce effects. A given stimulus provokes a given reaction, foreseeable and repetitive. As much as action is a matter of choice or, could one say, conscious obligation – that of responding to the truth of the moment – so does reaction proceed from non-choice, a mechanical obligation: the ego, governed by its conditioning, finds itself constrained to react, often against its own real interests. Existence pushes the buttons and the machine starts up, having no other option but to function the way it was programmed to do.

The Sovereign Mechanicality of the Devil's Children

For your Spiritual Enemy, the delectable aspect of this state of things resides in the fact that the machine believes itself to be autonomous; how delightful that a nonentity should dream of being a conscious subject! For your faithful adversary this is a constant source of wonderment: seeing Mr. Jones sincerely pretend to be exercising his sovereign liberty even when he finds himself utterly compelled to pronounce this or that word; Mrs. Jones thinking she's being rational and responsible even when she finds herself constrained to adopt this or that attitude ...

The dangerous Mr. Gurdjieff, an opponent who, long after his death is still causing much trouble for your Enemy, talked in his own peculiar French jargon of the "*merdité*" or "shit-ity" of the mechanical man; that appellation, admittedly hardly flattering, didn't come, as people believe – and as your Enemy did his best to make people believe – from any disdain for humanity; technically, it signified the inconsistency of a subject who has yet to appear. It's not a criticism of man, personally, but sheds a harsh light on the consistent lie of believing oneself unified when one is only a collection of spare parts.

In conclusion, everything being for the worst in the best of mechanical worlds, react! In other words, *always act on the spur of the emotion*. Carried away by your emotional blindness, declared or latent, commit "acts" whose justice is questionable and whose consequences you are later unwilling to face. Have you found a memo you don't agree with on your desk? Without the slightest deliberation, grab the phone and, in the heat of the moment, call the person who sent it. You received an unpleasant letter? Snatch up your pen or leap to the computer to impulsively compose a biting response. Has your spouse made a remark you find unpleasant? Bark your answer right back so s/he won't have the last word. Take every shortcut to do things as quickly as possible at the risk of regretting it the next day and having to undo what you thought was "done." Let emotion, good or bad, be your compass – everyone knows what befalls the traveler who tries to find his way with a broken compass. Venerate emotion as your only God, the potentate you will obey to the letter while denying his hold on you – "Me, carried away by emotional blindness? Not on your life!"

In short, let emotion be the criteria, the uncontested trigger of your deeds which, in this case, will always be reactions mistaken for actions.

For s/he who is doing his/her best to err on the path, lost reacting is optimally beneficial: the very fact of acting under the influence of emotion, manifest or latent, embodies that emotion, nourishes it, maintains it. An emotion that one observes, letting it rise then fall within oneself like a soufflé, is not objectified, while an emotion that is immediately and blindly expressed (or one should say "vomited"), instantly acquires more reality.

The key to failure on one's path consists of ceaselessly injecting reality into our illusions; reaction, from this point of view, proves to be a royal way.

Here's another considerable benefit: reaction prohibits all peace. The human being is indeed so constructed that despite all his mechanicality he remains, deep within himself, conscious of the fairness or unfairness of his behavior, whatever his surface denials and rationalizations. Undoubtedly this is due to that inviolable element once called the "conscience." A guarantee of a "bad conscience," reaction is thus a synonym for interior division.

Yet, as that agitator named Jesus once remarked, "What can a kingdom divided against itself do?"

In ineluctably fomenting division, reaction guarantees the pursuit of conflict and thus prevents the advent of peace. That is easily explained: an attempt to internally put things back into balance that springs from the need to release tension, reaction provokes an unbalancing at the same time as it rebalances. It only relieves one tension by simultaneously creating another.

Here's an example: Mrs. Jones makes a "little comment" to Mr. Jones, that little comment being the exact words likely to irritate him in the moment. Otherwise put, Mr. Jones mechanically refuses that his wife pronounce, at this particular moment, those particular words. On top of what is – moved by her own mechanicality, she is saying what she cannot not be saying – the mind superimposes something else. Over and against the one truth of what simply is, mind creates a second: a nice Mrs. Jones agreeing with whatever her husband does. This superimposition of a second on the one creates a gap that manifests itself as tension. Quite naturally, Mr. Jones experiences the imperious need to relieve the tension. Hence he reacts in a desperate attempt to regain the peace he's lost: he replies with his own rather nasty comment. This harsh response, although it does indeed relieve Mr. Jones' tension by allowing the energy accumulated by the gap to flow out, at the same time gives rise to new tensions, internal as well as external: external because the wife, highly insulted, counterattacks in one way or another – with aggression, tears, or sulking – her reaction then calling for another reaction from the husband; a reaction that will trigger a new reaction from the wife and so on and so forth, if not unto death, at least until, exhausted by this fruitless battle, the combatants cease their fire and negotiate a provisional peace treaty; internal for, at the very instant that he is relieved, the husband feels deep inside that his response to the situation is not appropriate. Whether he expresses it this way or not, he knows very well he hasn't acted but reacted. Unable to feel whole and unified in the reaction, he denies the very fact he's in the process of reacting – a denial that gets even more interesting thanks to the mental reference to spiritual teachings: "I am reacting right now, I shouldn't be reacting, I am not practicing, I'm worthless, I knew it, gotta say yes, can't, anyway it's her fault, it's too hard, why me?" etc.

Such is the law, the superb vicious circle: reaction only engenders reaction! As soon as he denies, Mr. Jones is divided. Thus divided, he reacts. The more he reacts, the blinder he becomes; the blinder he becomes, the more he reacts, his reactions gradually fuelling the reactions of the other. The more he reacts, the more divided he is; the more divided he is, the more he feels compelled to react in a desperate attempt to relieve his tension; the more he struggles with the crazy hope of relieving his tension by reacting, the more he gives rise to new tensions, etc., etc.

Thus blindly maintained, the endless chain of reactions constitutes one of the pillars of the unrestricted reign of your Enemy on an individual as well as a national scale. In the same way that countries, from retort to retort, from rejoinder to rejoinder, from vengeance to vengeance, mire themselves in interminable and bloody confrontations, human beings carried away by their mechanicality fuel their wars instant by instant.

In effect, taken far beyond the squabble between Mr. and Mrs. Jones, the logic of reaction is the logic of war, which is that of the ego, the source and fuel of all conflicts, both individual and collective.

Based on the impression of existing alone confronted by a threatening outside world, the ego only understands victory or defeat. Unable to conceive of true peace, the fruit of a vision anchored in the non-separation of the "self" and "the other," the ego neither conceives of, nor seeks, anything but its own peace, in other words, the triumph of its will. Perpetually in quest of security through flight or domination, the ego only reacts. Reaction is thus the very means of expression of this famous ego, the incarnation in each one of us of the Universal Enemy. If God actually did make man in his image, so did the Devil. He is reflected in you by the illusion of being an artificial, separate entity – a representation that is no less effective, seeing as it passes for the truth until it is exposed.

Take the large view. *Don't think that by reacting in your restricted sphere you content yourself with secreting your own unhappiness and that of those close to you. In truth, you do much more than that; you become part of nothing less than the sickness of the world.* Every time you act under the influence of emotion, you add a link to the chain of reactions and thus of unhappiness. You further consolidate that diabolical image which, in you as in each person, covers up the image of God.

You who strive to fail in the Way, continue to stock up the logic of reaction. You will thus become an artisan of war.

Emotional Diarrhea, Therapy-pee-pee and Anal-ysis

To persist in the way-with-no-exit, you'll need, of course, some justifications. You'll find them once again in the perversion of a truth. In order to legitimize your reactions, rely on a sensible notion – that is, that it's not good to bottle things up.

"I feel better now that I've said it," goes the popular expression, alternated with psychotherapeutic discourses which all insist, with reason, on the harmful effects of repression, family secrets, and the non-circulation of words. Make of this generally true affirmation a catechism that you'll indistinctly apply to all specific incidences. On the pretext that, yes, "one should talk rather than keeping things to oneself," never ask yourself who says what, to whom, when and how.

Always say everything that you feel like saying to everyone, especially if no one asks or, if they ask, it's in bad faith. Out of fear of repression seen as the absolute evil, consider that all truth – or what seems to be truth – is always worth saying. Reinforced by this conviction, at the slightest opportunity vomit your emotion on the other. Use him or her as a dumping ground for your emotional garbage. Become an adept of *emotional diarrhea*: like a child who can't control the movement of his innards, move on through life profusely vomiting your outbursts, positive or negative, always in the name of the sacrosanct "expression." You will be all the more inclined to adhere to this dogma if in your childhood you were severely reprimanded for it, as was often the case in the past, or, on the contrary, raised without rules, as is often the case today. Strictly brought up or spoiled, you're a candidate for chronic, emotional vomiting legitimized by a poorly assimilated, therapeutic catechism.

Push this perverted truth according to which one must always "say all" to the maximum, if possible with the aid of a therapy that insists on regression rather than structure. You'll have no trouble finding aid and support in this direction. A number of practicing therapists, more or less well-trained, have become (without knowing it) zealous servants of the Enemy, by retaining only half of the therapeutic process. Themselves having been damaged children, most often repressed, they see in the tireless expression of emotion the panacea for all ills. Even when sometimes expressed in pedantic terms, their logic is simple if not to say simplistic. It is based as always on a half-truth, a vision that's true but partial, erecting only an aspect of the totality: because the uneasiness experienced in adulthood stems from repressed, infantile emotions, the mere fact of getting back in touch with and expressing these emotions will permit one to get free from them. In their naïve zeal – the zeal that services naïve convictions being one of the Enemy's most devastating weapons – these therapists conveniently neglect the other and indispensable side of this coin, that is to say the building of an inner structure. The narcissism of these therapists benefits from that incomplete approach. Building an inner structure belongs to the paternal realm, having to do with limits, the law, the real. As such, it implies a certain solitude, whereas the maternal realm – that of fusion, of the "all possible," of the imaginary – perpetuates a connection that's very difficult to break. In permitting a child s/he's responsible for to integrate the paternal law, and thus to arrive at adulthood, the parent finds him or herself alone, given how true it is that the exercise of authority supposes that one assumes momentary rejection. In maintaining the child in the maternal law and thus in the infantile condition, the parent conserves an eternal hold. The therapists adept in regression only can be recognized notably by the fact that they have difficulty letting go of those patients with whom they find themselves locked in a co-dependant relationship. Invested by the patient with an abusive mother's power, a mother who imprisons her offspring in her skirts by retarding, as long as possible, his or her inevitable encounter with the law, the therapists rejoice, without admitting it, in feeling themselves monarchs of the psyche of others in a reign with no end.

There again, the contemporary context greatly favors

this confusion. It's one of the victories of your devoted Enemy to have established a society in which no one any longer knows the meaning of education: literally, it means "to lead out of." The manner in which the majority of pseudo-adults raise their children today proceeds from a reaction: from a style of education that resembled taming, they have lightheartedly gone onto untamed education. *From e-ducation, they go on to un-ducation.*

A number of mothers and fathers – under the pretext of no longer "repressing" their cherubs and, in truth, because, being infantile themselves, they dread rejection by their offspring – drop out as far as the transmission of the law is concerned.

Half of education – that which consists in accepting the child such as he is and respecting his rhythms and his needs – is, if not really applied, at least greatly claimed by those parents who dream about being perfect; the other half – that which demands one lead the child out of *his* world of all-powerfulness in order to introduce him into *the* world, a universe that no longer revolves exclusively around him, but within which, as an element of a whole, he occupies his rightful place – goes, on the contrary, more and more overlooked. The discourse destined to justify this dropping out tries, of course, to oppose these two halves, as if they could be dissociated, as if the unconditional acceptance of the child as he *is* wasn't the prerequisite to the imposition of fair limits as regards what he *does*.

From education / un-ducation erected as a norm in, not rehabilitative but redisabilitative therapy, there's but a step which you should quickly take. You'll then enter into the endless maneuvers of therapy-pee-pee or anal-ysis.

What needs to be avoided at all costs to assure you remain infantile, in other words, the slave of your emotions, is the acquisition of control.

For a long time your Enemy has delighted in seeing very young children ground down by educator-tamers demanding, too early and quickly, that the child be "toilet trained." The injunction to be toilet trained leads, quite naturally, once the sphincters are under control, to that of being "good." One will thus arrive at a model bambino, mouth closed and buttocks tightened, often convinced, deep down inside, that s/he is " shit," or, in any case, not the child s/he should be, that ideal child incessantly brandished by the parents, that unattainable perfection which must, nevertheless, be attained at all costs under penalty of seeing the indispensable love that's synonymous with life taken from him or her.

There was a disquieting time when one considered the baby as a person and the child as something other than a troublemaker who had to be put in his place "for his own good." The widespread influence of the likes of Françoise Dolto and Alice Miller caused a serious threat, but your Enemy regained his serenity when he saw to what extent the dimension of the law has been dropped in the current perception of the "new" education. Like the parents who, when the time comes, not only don't encourage the child to use the potty, but go so far as denying him access to it, the practitioners of therapy-pee-pee and anal-ysis maintain their patients in a regressed state where any kind of control is excluded. *The only God is emotion and expression is his prophet.* In this world where the child is king, the adult is a terrorist, a stupidly conformist and repressive figure, a torturer whose victims have every right to eternally denounce his abuse in a perpetual demand for damages with interest.

Not leading their patients toward the conscious control of emotional manifestations, these therapists block, as it were, their patients in the anal stage, that in which one not only defecates anytime, anywhere, but where one revels in wallowing in his pee-pee/caca soup.

Consequently, in order not to go beyond the stage of all powerful emotion and thus never grow up, be sure, in the name of "self development," to defecate your emotions anyhow, anytime, anywhere. Better yet, raise emotional diarrhea's value as proof of your progress along the path: "Aha, at forty-five I finally dared tell my seventy-year-old mother that I hate her and that she's a bitch! I warned my wife and children, 'Now that I'm working on myself, watch out, because I'm in a fighting mood!'" Reinforced by the legitimacy given by anal-ysis, plunge headlong into total regression.

Did Swami Prajnanpad present the path as a series of stages beginning with "only myself" and progressing to "myself and others," followed by "others and myself," and finally to "others only"? Have the courage to stay stuck at the "only myself" stage presented, not as the starting point, but as enormous progress. Let your credo be as simplistic as it is averse to building an inner structure: *evil is the non-expression of emotions, good is their expression.*

Thus consider as fair and good to be permanently on edge, ready to crack, and make it known. At the merest opportunity, scream, cry, stamp your feet. At thirty or forty, dump on others everything you couldn't manifest when you were three or four.

Become a savagely infantile adult. Impose this lawless persona on those closest to you on the pretext that, from now on, you're going "to finally be yourself." Make your family the hostages of the moods you vomit at all hours. It's your entire existence, and above all the domain called "private," that needs to transform itself into permanent, savage therapy. *Institute acting out – not seen as the transgression of a desperate child, but, on the contrary, rationalized as the action of an adult, as the ordinary relational mode.*

Avoidotherapy

Thus entrenched in chaos, you only need to persevere to go ever further toward confusion and, consequently, suffering.

The above-described anal-ysis and therapy-pee-pee find their fulfillment in a form of perpetual therapy that is assiduously practiced in spiritual circles. Your dear Enemy calls it *avoidotherapy.* An important factor in your failure on the path, avoidotherapy guarantees the ultimate objective of our proceedings, that is, the avoidance of any form of practice.

Avoidotherapy relies on a handful of simple postulates based, as always, on the principle of twisted truth. Being, in effect, neither totally false nor totally true, they prove to be, definitively, totally false, the Enemy's genius consisting of making the false appear to be true on the pretext that the false is only partially false.

Postulate number one: *The Way is based on practice but the latter is for the moment inaccessible to me because of my emotional blocks and other psychological "problems."* This postulate is partially true: certain disturbances and identifications do obscure vision; purifying the mind will contribute to sort things out and cleaning the windshield, so to speak. At the same time, the postulate is totally false: practice is for right now, and all purification of the mind undertaken without practice as the real goal will run up against its own limitations. Nevertheless, the postulate is very efficient in terms of avoidance: it's useless to attempt anything here and now as far as practice is concerned. The reason is understood: *practicing right away is impossible for me. First, I've got to "work on myself," "resolve my problems," "release my blocks." Oh yes, I'll practice ... later, when I've finished my therapy, completed my analysis, gone as far as possible in my "work on myself."*

Otherwise put, *psychological exploration is conjugated in the present tense, a fictitious present that stretches endlessly toward the promise of a radiant future, the psychotherapeutic Big Night where everything will, at last, be "settled"; while practice is conjugated in the future tense,* a vague and distant future, so distant that it is, to the path, what adulthood is to the child: purely imaginary, or more accurately, unimaginable, but where everything seems possible. There is only one small difference: if there is no eternal childhood, adulthood arriving sooner or later, barring an early death, there are endless therapies permitting one to stay at the same age all during the therapy without ever passing onto the era of the disciple.

In putting practice off until later, in conditioning it to some sort of psychological breakthrough, avoidotherapy accomplishes an infernal masterstroke: *it is the path that serves the therapeutic process rather than the therapeutic process that serves the path.*

We have here a superb example of diabolical logic: did Swami Prajnanpad recognize that, for most of his students, Westerners or Indians, the unconscious would necessarily have to be brought to light? Did Karlfried Graf Dürckheim direct his disciples toward Jungian analysis? Now that's the proof that it *is* best to *begin* by psychological work, and *then*, eventually, approach the distant shores of spirituality. This is a magnificent perversity that succeeds in making one lose sight of the end – the vertical positioning of practice here and now – by only seeing the means – a certain purification of the psyche. Avoidotherapy thus justifies itself by turning the path into a pretext for therapy. The supposed ultimate goal, therefore, is no longer anything more than the endorsement of a limited objective.

Postulate number two: *the past is an actual space.* Behind me runs my past, a linear zone where reside the causes of my current difficulties and inaptitude to practice. This leads us directly to the myth of the origin: there is a beginning that explains everything. My unease, here and now, is only the consequence of yesterday's uneasiness, that of my childhood or even my past lives. If, aboard the therapeutic time machine, I return to the past, I can easily change the course of the cause or causes. My life is a video film that I can rewind and then intervene in the cutting process to modify the scene or scenes of my choice.

Postulate number three: *it is not only possible, but desirable, to understand all, understanding being the key to control.* Your Enemy marvels to note, in the so-called spiritual seekers, the persistence of a scientific pretension that most of today's scientists have renounced, that of explaining the universe in order to better manipulate it. Would we really understand the mechanisms of the big bang – if big bang there was – it still would not give us any explanation of its source, which is to say, why there is something rather than nothing? Forgetting the obvious – that the most profound explanations, the most accurate comprehension, stop at the threshold of mystery – the adepts of avoidotherapy are driven by the crazy hope of being able to explain their universe and thus evacuate the mystery. A mystery that's very embarrassing for the ego whose motto is: *I understand, therefore I control.*

Ah, that old, never abandoned dream: to act on what is! The uneasiness I feel here and now shouldn't exist. It's obviously an error that I have every intention of rectifying. My goal is certainly not to be "one with" this uneasiness, but to become "one without it." In getting at the cause of this uneasiness, I'll achieve my goal: to ensure that "what is but doesn't suit me" no longer is.

As always, the Enemy's victory depends on the fuelling of a confusion between the existential and the essential, between the temporal plane and that of here and now.

In linear logic it's not only legitimate but necessary to seek the causes of an accident once it's happened in order to try to avoid it happening again in the future. One can certainly hope to prevent the repetition of unfortunate events provoked by the same identifiable causes. *The Enemy, therefore, lies not in the attempt at prevention but in the belief that prevention can be a control*, the absolute guarantee against future accidents.

The ego confuses action and control, mistakes the mere fact of doing what can be done for a guarantee of desired results. It acts as if one or several identifiable causes resulted, alone, in an effect; as if what happens at a given moment didn't happen as the result of a chain of infinitely complex causes, the great majority of which are not discernible and never will be; as if the linking of causes and effects could be entirely understood by our limited intelligence; as if here and now wasn't the domain of all possibility because of all the incomprehensible complexity of movements at work on the most obvious as well as the most subtle levels. In fact, accidents continue to happen despite legitimately taken precautions and despite whatever one can do to eliminate the causes.

Isn't a catastrophe – or a miracle, for that matter – precisely that most improbable of events which nevertheless and against all odds happens because of a conjunction, in itself unpredictable, of causes – some of which are detectable and others forever unknown?

The most stultifying lesson being that which one keeps endlessly repeating, the Enemy suggests you recapitulate the basics of avoidotherapy and copy them out one hundred times:

★ The past is a place. In the past resides the course of what exists today.

★ Because the past is a place, I'm going to go back there.

★ In going back, I'll see the causes of the present and thus understand what is.

★ By understanding, I'll control what is. I understand all, therefore I control.

★ In controlling, I'm free, free according to the ego: not with, but without; not pain without me, but me without pain.

Once these postulates are well-assimilated, you need only draw the concrete consequences: *let the search for "the" cause take the place of practice.* Be set in this decisive misunderstanding. It is the key to imaginary practice, since real practice resides not in the absolute power over what arises in me – whatever arises being part of what is here and now on which I am powerless– but over the relationship to what arises, the rapport established with whatever happens.

Thus, in order for your practice to remain in the imaginary realm, cultivate the "Why?" reflex. An unseemly thought comes to you, an inappropriate emotion gushes forth? Above all don't enter into direct relationship with those "errors." Seek to find out "what that refers to."

Begin by denying that thought, that emotion, which quite simply shouldn't arise. Entrenched in your denial of what, however, is in the instant, work at finding the cause. *An emotion? I want to know why.* As long as you pursue the why on the basis of denial, you'll be certain not to practice. Be like a driver who, skidding, asks himself, while his car runs headlong off the road, why this skid took place rather than trying, if possible, to bring the vehicle back into its axis; or like a practitioner of judo who, falling, wonders about the reasons for the fall rather than negotiating it.

There again, the true art of avoidance rests on an error in timing. Legitimate and eventually useful, once the emotion is appeased and vision returns, the quest for the deep reason of any disturbance and for its connections in the past blocks all real practice as soon as it's placed first, presented not as what's important, but as what is essential.

Do not feel what you are feeling here and now. Instead, intellectualize it and slap a nice "practice" label on that intellectualization.

As to real practice, don't give it a second's consideration. Don't imagine that whenever an emotion arises you can apply yourself to experiencing it entirely within yourself without repressing it but also without vomiting it out. Don't taste the emotion as you would a wine. *Don't let it have its full play in you and then vanish.* Never attempt that alchemist's process which consists of concentrating on the emotion as one concentrates, with certain meditation techniques, on the flame of a candle. Don't train yourself to savor whatever you are feeling, in other words, to have, for the first time, the full and entire experience of emotion that's usually denied, refused, or even annexed by the ego, in the case of an emotion experienced in a positive light.

Briefly put, avoid at all costs direct contact with emotion. Refuse to experience it while experiencing it anyway. Since in reality you can't separate yourself from what is, you'll thus experience that superb division that consists of insisting that you are not feeling what you are actually feeling, a division that manifests itself by a gust of thoughts which create even more emotion which will in turn secrete even more thoughts, etc.

Thus entrenched in the denial of emotion and launched heedlessly in the search for causes, you'll live under the definitive yoke of the past. Complain bitterly about that tyranny, but never question it. Don't foment the only revolution that's apt to overthrow it. Be the eternal victim of your personal history rather than its disciple. *Objectify your pain, erect a statue to it that you'll place in the center of your universe and in front of which you'll take care to prostrate yourself each morning.*

Let your sacrosanct pain become the object of your devotion, the unique and jealous God whose worship will mobilize all your energy. The mind being a museum whose conservator is named "me," put your bumps and scratches under glass. Piously preserve the relics of your infantile torments. In the super-production called, *My Tragedy*, isolate several major episodes (baptized "traumas") as so many cult scenes that you'll play over and over. Count off the rosary of your unhappiness, the litany of your suffering. Revive your passion by contemplating at length every station of your personal cross: station number one: me, frustrated by my mother; station number two: me, dethroned by my little sister; station number three, me: terrified by my father; and so on.

If you're the devotee of this sect, the priest will, of course, be the anal-yst or avoidotherapist with whose complicity you'll stay in eternal therapy. You can opt for the therapy-pee-pee mentioned above based on a flight backwards toward ever-further regression: "I'm still in pain because I didn't relive my birth, only found three past lives … " If the path you pretend to follow includes or offers some form of regressive work, place all your hopes in it. Don't take into consideration the fact that this work of purification, certainly necessary in most cases, only represents at best a quarter of the path, and can't in any case be dissociated from the whole practice. Become obsessed with that aspect, see it as a panacea. See all other practices as only a preparation, a prelude to serious things, an antechamber to the room where you can finally lie down on a mattress or punch a pillow in order to vomit your denial.

Frigitherapy and Abolitherapy

If you don't choose therapy-pee-pee or anal-ysis you can take recourse in another form of endless therapy, founded on the inverse principle, that of absolute frustration. Moreover, it's a joy to note that apparently opposite strategies arrive at the same result: non-progression on the path. With what one could call icy analysis, frozen therapy or frigitherapy, you will not be in backward flight; you will quite simply stand in place.

The principle is simple, the scenario well-worked: you go at a fixed day and time to a trained practitioner who is a firm tenant of distance, muteness, that clinical Siberia presented as a cure. This practitioner, generally a virtuoso of concept, often the author of articles that are perfectly unreadable for the unini-tiated, barely extends his aseptic hand to greet you upon your arrival or, as you leave, his icy fingertips to seize the bills you offer each time in exchange for his wintry presence, called "lis-tening." Having landed upon a couch behind which, out of your sight, sits the great professional, or finding yourself seated a good distance from him in an uptight face to face encounter, you will speak to an impassible physiognomy whose lips only move to signal, to the second, the end of the session. On the good days he'll perhaps prove more voluble and condescend to dissect, in a smooth voice, the manner in which you function, before he shows you out the door. That type of icy analysis can extend over ten, fifteen, twenty years or, why not, unto the death – yours or the analyst's. Above all, pay no attention to that handful of psycho-analysts who ruin the profession by still daring to insist that a "cure" can't last indefinitely.

Finally, one of the juicier strategies consists of *blocking* the most experienced of therapists, whether they're pee-pee, anal, refrigerated, obscure, mute, or, even better, quite simply competent and honest. One could call this abolitherapy. Successively try all the categories, consciously use every type. Begin with an initial appointment where you explain to the shrink how much his or her predecessor disappointed you and that you feel that, with him or her, on the other hand, work can really, at last, begin. If the therapist falls into your trap and accepts you as a patient – provided s/he doesn't accept you knowing what you're up to through pure compassion, a dose of greed or the somewhat naive conviction that s/he'll succeed where the others have failed – consult with him or her a few times to save face and make yourself believe that you really tried to accomplish something. Then, after a few sessions, decree that nothing is happening, that you're going in circles; make a show of being shocked by the therapist's attitude, find s/he's got faults or an inaptitude you simply can't get around, and tranquilly return to your status of all-powerful victim for whom no one, not even the best, or reputed to be so, can do anything.

Lifetherapy

If you tire of giving as much money to shrinks as you do to the tax collector, you can always cross the barrier and become a therapist yourself in order to pursue your eternal therapy through that of your patients. Perhaps all these efforts will lead you to the state of lifetherapy, that state where therapy and existence become one. Does one of Shakespeare's characters see life as, "a tale told by an idiot, full of sound and fury, signifying nothing"? *Let your life be nothing but a therapy, uttered by a patient, full of whining and complaints leading to nothing at all.*

Above all, *consider that emotion precedes thought, not the reverse.* Now that you can't seem to talk about anything besides emotion, and are reducing the path to a supposed "emotional work," don't in the least consider that aspect of the practice which has to do with paying attention to one's thought process. You couldn't care less about the vigilance that's indispensable for training oneself to that aspect and thus to practice. Practice for you will be summed up as "trying not to have emotions any longer" even as you complacently wallow in them day after day. Your money, your time, your energy will be invested in endless therapy devoid of perspective, the eternal quest for the miracle training-program or new technique. The years will pass without your practicing. Not practicing, you'll grow old without having matured. Everything will be for the best in the most diabolical of all possible worlds. Thanks to this vain and sterile obsession with the emotional, you'll have achieved the goal: *avoidance of practice.*

6

The Power to Say No

I Refuse, Therefore I Am

Every second has its no.
—The Spiritual Enemy

Dear spiritual seeker, hypocritical seeker, my other self, my
brother ...

To wind things up, we are going to get to the essential, to
the secret of secrets, to the initiative key, your permanent access
card to the infernal kingdom, your ultimate guarantee to never
ever reach paradise.

Dear seeker determined never ever to find, know that,
should all other strategies fail, should the worst happen, should
the collection of ruses, perversions and detours previously
detailed be somehow defeated, despite everything, you always
have one prerogative left. Only one, perhaps, but oh how formi-
dable, decisive, radical: the power to say no.

When I Hear the Word Yes, I Pull out My Gun

In a book entitled *Anthology of Non Duality*, a work to be
avoided at all costs, some French author, Véronique Loiseleur,
demonstrated, with an erudite assemblage of quotes issuing from
all traditions, to what extent "yes" not only is a constant from the
spiritual perspective, but defines it and even constitutes its

essence.

Whether one calls it submission to the divine will, abandoning oneself to providence, letting go, presence in the here and now, vision of the real, acceptance of what is, non-duality, non-separation, surrender, this non resistance to what is establishes the mystical attitude.

This attitude has, fortunately, become incomprehensible and unimaginable. In a society where revolt and righteous indignation have been promoted to values, in which the obsession of control reigns to the point where every accident or apparent whim of nature is perceived as a personal offence to the victims and their families, where the mere evocation of an eventual "submission" is seen as an insult to both one's good sense and dignity, acceptance no longer has its place. Relegated to the back room of bankrupt religions – which having lost sight of its meaning only refer to it in the form of weak and wearisome sermons stripped of all credibility – acceptance is covered with such a thick coat of misunderstanding, mixed signals and incomprehension that it's become inconceivable.

Therefore, everything is for the best in the most senseless of all possible worlds and your Enemy sleeps the sweet sleep of the wicked. Nevertheless, knowing once again that a well-informed non-practitioner is worth two, here are a few clarifications destined to counteract the improbable influence of a living teaching.

Being One Without

First, let's get to the essence of non-practice. What do you need to do, what interior gesture must you accomplish, moment after moment, to be sure to stay in *your* world without ever gaining access to *the* world? Truth be told, this gesture is terrifyingly simple. It's a matter of merely denying the obvious.

At every instant, here and now, from the time you awaken, in the most elementary sense of the term – it's understood that this means you're not sleeping, haven't fainted or fallen into a coma – a collection of physical, emotional and mental perceptions present themselves to your consciousness. You are conscious of certain physical sensations, of the emotional nuances of the moment – ill at ease, ecstatically happy, desperate, or simply relaxed – of some of your thoughts; and you are conscious of what can best be called the "exterior" – that which, in reality, arises in you from the simple fact that you are. The eyes see, the ears hear, all the senses function; you perceive and then interpret, according to your conditioning, the data coming to you at that instant.

All these experiences, including of course eventual thoughts and representations relative to another place and another time, constitute your experience here and now. Your experience, in any case, is equivalent to *what is here and now*, for you; *what is* being only conjugated in the present tense: thoughts about the past and future arrive *now*, and those concerning another place are coming to *you here*.

Thus, here and now, you are relating to your experience, in other words, to what is. In fact you are connected to it. Whether the experience be pleasant or unpleasant, you are no more separated from it than you are from your own breathing which, moreover, is part of it. Thus you are connected, in relationship with. *You are, in reality, one with*.

For example, if you find yourself at this very instant in the process of reading theses lines, you can no more separate yourself from that precise aspect of your experience than you can from all the others. It's up to you, in this case, to take what action you can. But nothing and no one can, in the instant, modify what is, or change the fact that, at this precise moment, you are deciphering these words, perceiving this book in your line of vision, as well as being taken up by all the facets of this present experience.

Thus, here and now, what is is and you are in no way separated from it. You don't exist independently of the whole, you don't control it. To control, one must be outside and not part of. What is is here and now, the unique result of an assembly of causes and effects of which you are an element, but which is totally beyond you. Not only can't you intervene in what is in the moment, but your very action in time, as important and necessary as it might be, remains limited because it also submits to the imperatives of the whole.

In other words, if, as a human being, it's your place to act, the action is in no way a control. In your capacity as an integral part of the whole, you control nothing. Anything can happen at any moment and your action inserts itself into the fathomless and uncontrollable chain of cause and effects.

The procedure to follow in order to maintain yourself under the grip of illusion is disconcertingly simple. Denying the reality that you indeed are one with, one with what is – your present experience in all its aspects – insist on being one without. Such and such an aspect of your experience in the moment doesn't please you? Insist on being able to separate yourself from it here and now.

Apply this foolish, absurd, senseless, pretension – that is nevertheless obvious for the mind – to every moment; to the most ordinary as well as the most extraordinary circumstances. Do you feel tired? Deny it. Deny the connection that nevertheless unquestionably unites you, in the present moment, to that sensation. Insist that you are in the instant without that sensation you find unpleasant, *as if you could suddenly extract yourself from the whole*. Upon this sensation, the only immediate reality, superimpose what, according to you, should be, an impression of being full of energy. Over the one reality, the sensation of fatigue, stick a second – me full of energy. *Not what is, but what should be. Refuse the fact that what is is. On the one truth that is, superimpose a second truth entirely fabricated by the mind.*

Please do not underestimate that method of non-practice: by refusing that what is is, denying the connection which links you to your present experience, you are not merely grumbling, ranting and raving, or revolting: *you are reactivating nothing less than the very principle of separation, the inmost essence of illusion. At every instant, just like that, as if it were nothing, you assert yourself as a separate entity supposedly independent of the whole, capable of intervening in what is and thus of controlling the universe. In short, you take yourself for God.* Hypnotized by your fears, desires and attachments, entrenched in *your* world, guarded against *the* world, you persist in a remarkably ridiculous presumption: the presumption to substitute yourself for the divine.

Know that whatever your efforts, spiritual disciplines, exercises, experiences, prayers, benedictions, realizations, purifications, meditations and comprehensions, you will remain in the Enemy's power as long as you don't have the disastrous idea to convert the rejection into adhesion. The mechanism of rejection being a constituent of the ego, the separated me, you need only perpetuate it to be certain never to question that "me." *I refuse, therefore I am. And as long as I reject, I am.*

Every Second Has its No

It's marvelous to see, oh hypocritical seeker, to what extent you pretend to be in quest of the "Real," the "One without a Second" exalted in the Upanishads, the "here and now"; how much you enjoy going on and on about "non-separation" without ever glimpsing that those glorious concepts could relate to your ordinary, day to day experience. Be sure not to change that attitude. Above all, *establish no connection between non-duality and daily life*. Keep it in the lofty spheres of Hindu metaphysics without suspecting it has the merest relation to accepting, here and now, the fact that the elevator does not arrive. Endlessly comment on non-separation at the same time that you spend your days intent on separating yourself from what is. Adoringly listen to talks about the One without a Second and then, as you are leaving the conference hall, superimpose yesterday's sunny sky on the rainy horizon.

There is something truly marvelous about this non-practice: not only is it simple, it is also innate – nothing simpler for the ego – and applicable to every moment regardless of the circumstances. *Every second has its no* and you will always find a pretext for refusing. Even if no aspect of your present experience disagrees with you, even if everything seems perfect, reflexively quit the plenitude of the present moment by thinking that it could no longer be, could not be at all, will necessarily cease to be – thoughts that will immediately result in a refusal, thus in a separation, instantly re-establishing you in your indignity as a stressed-out tiny self.

The surest way to never attempt the merest conversion is to not be truly conscious of the phenomenon and its actual proportions. Intellectually adhere to an exalting mystical teaching about the yes; admit, for show, that sometimes you enter into conflict with what is; but do not, in any way, try to size up the mechanism. Do not realize that refusal establishes you as a separated self and that, as such, you are constantly, moment by moment, occupied with refusing.

Don't conceive of the practical possibility of an infinitely repeated, interior gesture. Let all that remain vague, hazy, approximate.

Certainly never suspect that Christ could have alluded to this intimate disposition of non-resistance to what is when he advised "turning the other cheek," an incomprehensible, grotesque, even despicable attitude as long as it is seen in the ordinary perspective.

A Touch of Weakness

Precisely because acceptance is unacceptable on the ordinary level, it's important to maintain it there, to never glimpse its esoteric dimension.

In fact, it's a matter of remaining anchored in a misunderstanding; to base the entire way you enter into relation with life and the path on a misconception. Do spiritual teachings advocate the "yes," acceptance of what is, acquiescence to the divine will as it is manifested here and now? Very well. In order to turn this "yes" into a dangerous absurdity, you need only put it out of the moment, place it in time, and by the same stroke turn it into the antithesis of action.

As always, the trick is to take a truth, in itself integrally true on a given level, and then pretend to apply it to another level where, ceasing to be true, it becomes a lie. There again it's necessary to confuse the horizontal plane with the vertical plane, that of existence with essence.

Let the yes to what is here and now become, through a mental disappearing act, the impossibility of saying no in time, and, consequently, of acting, based on this no. In this famous yes, see not the letting go, in the moment, of the unreal and the return to the real, but the negation of all positioning, the defeat of reason and good sense, an attitude against nature that's exactly opposite to what founds the human being.

In fact, man's existential dignity relies in great part on the possibility of saying "no," his capacity to mobilize intelligence and energy in order to attempt to change what can be changed. *As an aptitude for not tolerating a state of things* felt to be intolerable, the "no" determines action.

How many noble and courageous acts, how many heroic stances, how many lifesaving initiatives, from the most extraordinary to the most ordinary, have proceeded from this power to say no?

Isn't General de Gaulle famous for being "he who said no"? Aren't the doctor saving a human life, the union leader rejecting wretched working conditions, or the father giving his son structure and security those who know how to say "no" and dare to translate this "no" into action?

In order to better avoid the converting inner gesture of the "yes," operated on the essential plane, always come back to the existential plane. Note the obvious, that is, that the "no" is indispensable to leading one's life, and go no further without ever glimpsing the fact that the "yes" exalted by the mystics is situated in an altogether different dimension. In other words, *confuse "accepting" with "tolerating."* In letting go, do not see anything but weakness; in adhesion to what is, fatalism; in submission, giving up. *Turn acceptance, that passively active disposition, into resignation, a passively passive disposition.* Make no distinction between mystical acceptance, an acquiescence to what is in the moment, and inertia when faced with the demands of existence. Can the essence of the spiritual attitude be summed up in two words: "accepting" and "acting"? Forget the second one. Pretend that practicing on the path only consists of "accepting." The cause is understood: it's not a matter, things being what they are, of seeing what can be done and then acting. It's a matter of compliantly noting the state of things the better to resign yourself to them.

Clearly, *everything relies on this confusion between acceptance and resignation.* Once well anchored in it, you need only opt for one or several of the diverse dead ends to which this starting point leads.

You can simply sweep away the mystical ways with the back of your reason by denouncing its fatalism – proof, if need be, that it is indeed that opium used by the governing classes to maintain the masses in an opportune inertia.

Nevertheless, it is much more fun to adhere in principle to the teaching of acceptance in order to pervert its practical meaning and arrive at a caricature.

An Elegy to the False Yes

Following the same logic become an adept of the "yes, but ... " Floundering about in the haziest of conceptions of yes, pretend to apply it while being, deep inside, convinced of the absurdity as well as the practical impossibility of this positioning. Confronted by all that troubles you, saddens you, irritates you, or even revolts you, bleat a shaky "yes." You've vaguely grasped that, according to the spiritual master, it's "necessary to say yes"? Well then, say yes in a weak, mournful, whining tone. Compliantly repeat, "yes … yes … I'm saying yes … gotta say yes … " like others repeat the "Our Father" or abracadabra, these murmurs skimming along your surface, while just underneath you are wholeheartedly refusing. This non-practice immediately causing you to note the foolishness of "yes," you will be obliged to pair it with a "but" followed by the enumeration of all your reasons to "say no," most of which, moreover, will be good reasons, the "yes" once more being, from the start, envisioned in a linear perspective where it remains not only inapplicable but absurd. By only envisioning the "yes" in the confines of your usual perspective, that's to say at the periphery of yourself, you will psychologize it and in fact annul it.

Let's imagine that you are waiting for a loved one at the airport and do not see him or her surge from the crowd of arriving passengers. In vertical, non-psychological acceptance, you need merely cease to pretend to separate yourself from what is: here and now, people are deplaning and I don't see X among them. The question is not to think about the inconveniences caused by a possible delay, to imagine X dead, injured or having missed the plane, but first and foremost in the instant to return to what is, over which the mind insists on superimposing what, according to it, should be. Vertical acceptance quite simply doesn't enter into linear considerations. These come later, and consciously, on the basis of non-discussion of the obvious. In horizontal acceptance, on the contrary, you need, immediately and mechanically, to think, interpret, qualify, project yourself into the past, the future, then stick a weak-willed yes on top of this foundation of psycho-emotional balderdash: "Yes, X isn't here; yes, perhaps, s/he's missed the plane, though I was so excited about seeing him/her and went to so much trouble to fix a special dinner; yes, something might have happened to him/her; yes, I'm going to have to wait here until midnight; yes, yeeess … " Having accomplished this mental marvel, you no longer even attempt to accept what is, but rather what you've substituted for what is – your thoughts – which you already have resolutely rejected. Therefore it's useless to continue, and this pseudo-attempt will only reinforce your conviction of the impossibility of all practice. And if the master or one of his colleagues attempts to sell you on the benefits of this famous yes, you'll hear yourself proffering this heartfelt cry, the pure fruit of the initial confusion between acceptance and resignation: "Yes, but, after all, one can't just accept everything!"

You can also become an adept at the yes-lid. The recipe is simple: take hold of a poorly assimilated yes in order to legitimize your tendency for flight, your penchants for inertia, and screw a lid on everything that might trouble your "peace." Pour a layer of pseudo-acceptance cement on the shifting ground of your most deeply buried emotions and refusals. Adopt a beatific smile and, in face of all contrariety minor or major, mechanically repeat "Yes, it is," before returning to your nebulous meditation or plunging your nose back in the newspaper. You'll thus advance through life covered with a veneer of "yes" that will confer an aspect of civility to you.

Lastly, as a refinement to perversity, *refuse* – on the pretext that you must accept. *In the name of the yes, say no.* Does the teaching you pride yourself on following sing the praises of acceptance? By one of those twists and turns the mind alone is capable of, turn acceptance into *what should be and yet is not.* Have you caught yourself in the act of flagrant denial? Well, there's a good reason for another refusal. Not of what is – here and now I am experiencing a no – but of what should be: I should accept, there should be a yes. *Over this one truth – the "no in the moment," superimpose a second in the form of an imaginary yes.* In the name of acceptance, refuse the no as an aspect of the whole.

Decide that from now on you'll be nothing but "yes," only and ever yes. You'll thus guarantee that you become ever more entrenched in the no since you can do no more than notice you are not saying yes. Don't deviate from your deviation: "I can't, in any case, be one with the fact that I'm not one with when I should be!"

By anchoring yourself in this position, you'll prohibit yourself from all real practice here and now. The unconditional peace you insist on seeking will perpetually be placed under a condition, always put off until later, even if that's for an additional, hypothetical second. The will of the Enemy who art in hell will be thus: he'll give you your daily refusals and it is to him that will belong the kingdom, the power and the glory forever and ever.

7

Seek, Do Not Find

Destined for disciples, the spiritual path is indeed a discipline. However, belonging to the subtle dimension, it has the advantage of permitting the unrestricted reign of the imaginary.

Let's imagine the weight room of a gym where a good number of the regulars sit around devouring *Flex* and *Muscle and Fitness*, pass their time conversing about weights and dumbbells, ask the trainers question after question about the comparative benefits of the "regular bench press," the "inclined bench press," and the "pull over" as regards developing the pectorals, and try out various protein drinks and energy snacks, without ever, or at least so rarely, pumping an ounce of iron. It's an incongruous vision, that gym where the majority of members, even after years of assiduous attendance, are ninety pound weaklings and where the practice sessions consist of putting on one's nicest sweats in order to sit and admire a very patient muscle man while asking him to explain the meaning of power, to reveal the exact nature of suppleness, or to give them the formula that will allow them, overnight, to pump 200 pounds.

However, this is the bizarre reality in ashrams, monasteries and centers dedicated to the quest for the essential. The path remains, to the immense pleasure of your beloved Spiritual Enemy, the only enterprise in which it is not only possible but customary to devote, *in appearance,* lots of time, energy and money without obtaining any results, except perhaps that of complicating what should be simple, and adding a thick coat of esoteric pretension to one's usual armor.

The search called "spiritual" is a club that has become increasingly popular, in which there is a concentration of professional seekers who seek without ever finding, and professional finders pretending to have found without ever seeking, yet always ready to teach their non-search to veteran seekers – who love to hear someone tell them, again and again, that while they think they haven't found, in fact they *have* actually *already* found, since, in any case, there isn't anything to seek in the first place.

The author of this book hopes to have formulated some of the implicit rules applied by the fervent members of this club – to which every seeker, no matter how sincere s/he is, immediately finds him/herself a member without having to apply, and often without his or her knowledge.

We all know the name or names of the Devil – Satan, the Evil Spirit, the mind, illusion, ignorance being some of them. What puzzles us, as he so well puts it himself in The Rolling Stones' song "Sympathy for the Devil," is the nature of the game he plays. Knowing the rules permits one to get around them. If persevering in error proves diabolical, each error in itself is not only human, but, as soon as it is identified and rectified, constitutes a step on the staircase of the truth. This conviction presided over the writing of what could also be called: *How to Fail on the Spiritual Path.*

APPENDIX A

The following spiritual teachers or authors have been mentioned in this text.

Ammachi (full name: Amritanandamayi Ma) (born 1952) – Like Ananda Mayi Ma (see below), Ammachi was filled with Divine wisdom from birth. She tirelessly travels the world dispensing her grace and healing through presence and loving embrace to all who approach her. Hailed widely as "the love of the God in human form" (Dr. Jane Goodall).

Ananda Mayi Ma (1896-1982) – Filled with Divine wisdom from birth, this much-loved Indian spiritual guide was regarded by people throughout the world as a manifestation of the Divine Mother.

Ramesh Balsekar (born 1919) – A former Indian bank president, now recognized as a contemporary sage and a master of pure Advaita teaching.

Jacques Castermane – After studies at the University of Brussels, he became the disciple of Karl Graf Dürckheim (see below) and remained in touch with him for more than twenty years. He is currently director of the Dürckheim Center, Drôme, France, carrying on the work based on three factors: recognition of numinous experiences, meditative exercises (zazen, silent sitting), and Jung's depth psychology.

Chandra Swami (born 1930) – With an ashram located in the remote Himalayas, this silent sage teaches by his profound spiritual presence. Many of his teachings – via written answers to questions of visitors and disciples – have been recorded in the book *Song of Silence*.

Andrew Cohen (born 1955) – An American spiritual teacher, founder and guide of the Impersonal Enlightenment Foundation and publisher of the popular magazine *What Is Enlightenment*.

Karlfried Graf Dürckheim (1896-1988) – One of Europe's most highly-respected and influential spiritual teachers of the 20th century. During his service in World War II in Japan he met masters of traditional disciplines (such as Zazen and bow practice) and was initiated by them. Combining Zen with Jungian psychology, he founded a center in Germany that attracted thousands of seekers over decades. His most famous book is *Hara*.

Francis of Assisi (1181-1226) – This son of a rich cloth merchant misspent his youth as a street brawler and some-time soldier. During an imprisonment he had a conversion experience after which he took the Gospels as the rule of his life, Jesus Christ as his literal example. He dressed in rough clothes, begged for his sustenance, and preached purity and peace. He began to attract followers in 1209, and thus founded the Franciscans.

Kangyur Rinpoche (1897-1975) (full name: Longchen Yeshe Dorje, Kangyur Rinpoche), of the monastery of Riwoche in Kham, was a great scholar and tertön (one who discovers hidden texts which have been concealed by great teachers of the past in various ways, until the time when they could be understood and applied). He left Tibet in the 1950s and was one of the first Tibetan masters to accept Western disciples.

Lee Lozowick (born 1943) – The spiritual son of Yogi Ramsuratkumar, Lee Lozowick is the founder and director of the Hohm Community, with ashrams in U.S., France and India. He is the author of numerous books, including thousands of devotional poems in honor of his Master. A representative of the Baul tradition in the West, Lee's teaching is called "spiritual slavery" as well as "enlightened duality."

Milarepa (1052-1136) – One of the most widely known Tibetan saints. In a superhuman effort, he rose above the misguided ways of his younger life and with the help of his Guru, Marpa the Translator, took to a solitary life of meditation until he had achieved the pinnacle of the enlightened state.

Richard Moss – A contemporary physician, author, and internationally-respected teacher of consciousness, who conducts retreats and seminars. His most popular books include: *The I That is We*, and *The Black Butterfly*.

Ramana Maharshi (1879-1950) – A world-renowned spiritual master whose awakening into non-dual consciousness was precipitated by a method of enquiry using the question, "Who am I?"

Ramdas (Swami Papa Ramdas) (1884-1963) – Born as Vittal Rao to a devout Hindu couple in Kerala, India, he led the life of a householder until the age of thirty-six. Having endured the trials of life in the world, he was overcome, in 1920, with a passionate yearning to realize his Divine nature. His means of liberation was to see all as Ram (God), and to chant constantly the mantra "Om Sri Ram Jai Ram Jai Jai Ram."

Shankara (788? - 820?) – Philosopher and theologian; born in southern India. He became a Hindu ascetic and exponent of the Advaita Vedanta school of philosophy. Shankara reformed Hinduism with a monistic interpretation of the Vedanta, which ascribed all reality to a single unitary source, which he identified as "Brahma." He declared all plurality and differentiation as nothing but an illusion.

Teresa of Avila (1515-1582) – This visionary, mystical writer and activist saint was born in Avila, Castile, Spain. She entered a monastery of Carmelite renunciates at seventeen. She considered her original convent too lax in its rule, so she founded a reformed convent and went on to serve as reformer of monasticism in her day, aided in her work by St. John of the Cross. In 1970 she was proclaimed a Doctor of the Church.

Irina Tweedie – (1907-1999) A Russian-born woman, living in England, who found her teacher (the Indian master she called Bhai Sahib) late in her life (at 54). After five years of intense training she was sent back to England to guide others. She attracted students worldwide, primarily through the biographical account of her sadhana, *Daughter of Fire*.

Yogi Ramsuratkumar (1918-2001) – An educated man who lived completely surrendered to God, as a beggar on the streets of southern India, after his awakening at the hands of Swami Papa Ramdas of Anandashram in 1952. His creed was "only God," and he credited all things to the Infinite Beneficence of God, whom he affectionately called "Father in heaven."

RECOMMENDED READING

The following short list of books may prove helpful to those in search of a genuine spiritual path:

Caplan, Mariana, *Do You Need a Guru?* London: Thorsens, 2002.

Caplan, Mariana, *Halfway Up the Mountain*. Prescott, Arizona: Hohm Press, 2001.

Desjardins, Arnaud, *The Jump into Life – Moving Beyond Fear*. Prescott, Arizona: Hohm Press, 1994.

Desjardins, Arnaud, *Towards the Fullness of Life – the Fullness of Love*. Prescott, Arizona: Hohm Press, 1993.

Fedorschak, VJ, *The Shadow on the Path: Clearing the Psychological Blocks to Spiritual Life*. Prescott, Arizona: Hohm Press, 1999.

Gurdjieff, George: any of his books, including: *Beelzebub's Tales to His Grandson; Life is Real Only Then, When "I Am"; Meetings with Remarkable Men*. Also, the related works of P.D. Ouspensky, which detail the teachings of Gurdjieff: including, *In Search of the Miraculous* and *The Fourth Way*.

Lozowick, Lee, *The Alchemy of Transformation*. Prescott, Arizona: Hohm Press, 1996.

Trungpa, Chögyam, *Cutting Through Spiritual Materialism*. Boston: Shambhala, 1973.

Tweedie, Irina, *Daughter of Fire*. Inverness, Calif.: The Golden Sufi Center, 1986.

Young, M., *As It Is – A Year on the Road with a Tantric Teacher*. Prescott, Arizona: Hohm Press, 2000.

INDEX

OTHER TITLES OF INTEREST FROM HOHM PRESS

AS IT IS
A Year on the Road with a Tantric Teacher
by M. Young

A first-hand account of a one-year journey around the world in the company of a *tantric* teacher. This book catalogues the trials and wonders of day-to-day inter-actions between a teacher and his students, and presents a broad range of his teachings given in seminars from San Francisco, California to Rishikesh, India. As It Is considers the core principles of *tantra*, including non-duality, compassion (the Bodhisattva ideal), service to others, and transformation within daily life. Written as a narrative, this captivating book will appeal to practitioners of any spiritual path. Readers interested in a life of clarity, genuine creativity, wisdom and harmony will find this an invaluable resource.

paper, 725 pages, 24 b&w photos, $29.95   ISBN: 0-934252-99-8

HALFWAY UP THE MOUNTAIN
The Error of Premature Claims to Enlightenment
by Mariana Caplan

Dozens of first-hand interviews with students, respected spiritual teachers and mas-ters, together with broad research are synthesized here to assist readers in avoiding the pitfalls of the spiritual path. Topics include: mistaking mystical experience for enlightenment; ego inflation, power and corruption among spiritual leaders; the question of the need for a teacher; disillusionment on the path . . . and much more. "Caplan's illuminating book . . . urges seekers to pay the price of traveling the hard road to true enlightenment."—*Publisher's Weekly*

paper, 600 pages $21.95   ISBN: 0-934252-91-2

THE WAY OF FAILURE: Winning Through Losing
by Mariana Caplan

This straight-talking and strongly inspirational book looks failure directly in the face, unmasking it for what it really is. Mariana Caplan tells us to how to meet fail-ure on its own field, how to learn its twists and turns, its illusions and its realities. Only then, she advises, is one equipped to engage failure as a means of ultimate "winning," and in a way that far exceeds our culturally defined visions of success.

paper; 144 pages; $14.95   ISBN: 1-890772-10-6

TO ORDER: 800-381-2700, or visit our website: www.hohmpress.com

OTHER TITLES OF INTEREST FROM HOHM PRESS

THE WOMAN AWAKE
Feminine Wisdom for Spiritual Life
by Regina Sara Ryan

Through the stories and insights of great women whom the author has met or been guided by in her own journey, this book highlights many faces of the Divine Feminine: the silence, the solitude, the service, the power, the compassion, the art, the darkness, the sexuality. Read about: the Sufi poetess Rabia (8th century) and contemporary Sufi master Irina Tweedie; Hildegard of Bingen, author Kathryn Hulme (*The Nun's Story*), German healer and mystic Dina Rees, and others. Includes personal interviews with contemplative Christian monk Mother Tessa Bielecki; artist Meinrad Craighead and Zen teacher and anthropologist Joan Halifax.

paper; 20 photos; 518 pages; $19.95   ISBN: 0-934252-79-3

THE SHADOW ON THE PATH
Clearing the Psychological Blocks to Spiritual Development
by VJ Fedorschak
Foreword by Claudio Naranjo, M.D.

Tracing the development of the human psychological shadow from Freud to the present, this readable analysis presents five contemporary approaches to spiritual psychotherapy for those who find themselves needing help on the spiritual path. Offers insight into the phenomenon of denial and projection.

Topics include: the shadow in the work notable therapists; the principles of inner spiritual development in the major world religions; examples of the disowned shadow in contemporary religious movements; and case studies of clients in spiritual groups who have worked with their shadow issues.

paper, 300 pages, 6 x 9; $17.95   ISBN: 0-934252-81-5

A MAN AND HIS MASTER: My Years With Yogi Ramsuratkumar
by Mani, with S. Lkasham

A personal account by Yogi Ramsuratkumar's trusted "right-hand man," Mani, of his six years at the master's side. Mani's heart and extraordinary faith shine through this touchingly personal and intimate account.

paper, 394 pages, $21.95   ISBN: 1-890772-36-2

TO ORDER: 800-381-2700, or visit our website: www.hohmpress.com

OTHER TITLES OF INTEREST FROM HOHM PRESS

YOGI RAMSURATKUMAR: Under the Punnai Tree
by M. Young

Hohm Press's first full-length biography of the wondrous and blessed beggar of Tiruvannamalai, Yogi Ramsuratkumar. This comprehensive yet personal account contains firsthand interviews, anecdotes and teaching stories that demonstrate a life that is mystical and astounding in its scope, while at the same time felt to be "nearer than near." To read this book is to meet a saint!

paper, 826 pages, 80+ photos, $39.95   ISBN: 1-890772-34-8

FACETS OF THE DIAMOND: Wisdom of India
By James Capellini

A book of rare and moving photographs, brief biographies, and evocative quotes from contemporary spiritual teachers in the Eastern tradition, including Ramana Maharshi, Swami Papa Ramdas, Sri Yogi Ramsuratkumar, Swami Prajnanpad, Chandra Swami, Nityananda, Shirdi Sai Baba, and Sanatan Das Baul. This mood-altering book richly captures the texture and flavor of the Eastern spiritual path and the teacher-disciple relationship, and offers penetrating insight into the lives of those who carry the flame of wisdom for the good of all humanity.

cloth, 240 pages, $39.95, 45 b&w photographs   ISBN: 0-934252-53-X

ONLY GOD: A Biography of Yogi Ramsuratkumar
by Regina Sara Ryan
Foreword by Jay Martin, Ph.D.

A full-length biography of the contemporary saint Yogi Ramsuratkumar (1918-2001), also known as the Godchild of Tiruvannamalai, who spent his days as a beggar on the streets of South India and graced all who met him with his unforgettable humor, kindness and blessing force. "Only God" was his creed and his approach to daily life.

cloth, 832 pages, 30+ photos, $39.95   ISBN: 1-890772035-6

TO ORDER: 800-381-2700, or visit our website: www.hohmpress.com

Hohm Press Retail Order Form

Name _____ Phone (____) _____

Street Address or P.O. Box _____

City _____ State _____ Zip Code _____

QTY	TITLE	ITEM PRICE	TOTAL
	AS IT IS	29.95	
	HALFWAY UP THE MOUNTAIN	21.95	
	THE WAY OF FAILURE	14.95	
	THE ALCHEMY OF TRANSFORMATION	14.95	
	THE ALCHEMY OF LOVE AND SEX	16.95	
	ZEN TRASH	12.95	
	THE YOGA TRADITION	29.95	
	THE JUMP INTO LIFE	12.95	
	TOWARD THE FULLNESS OF LIFE	12.95	
	THE WOMAN AWAKE	19.95	
	THE SHADOW ON THE PATH	17.95	
	A MAN AND HIS MASTER	21.95	
	YOGI RAMSURATKUMAR	39.95	
	FACETS OF THE DIAMOND	39.95	
	ONLY GOD	39.95	
	THE ANTI-WISDOM MANUAL	14.95	

SUBTOTAL: _____

SHIPPING: _____
(See Below)

TOTAL: _____

SURFACE SHIPPING CHARGES:
1st book or tape item........$5.00   Each additional item add $1.00

SHIP MY ORDER:
☐ Surface U.S. Mail—Priority   ☐ Fed-Ex Ground (Mail + $3.00)
☐ 2nd Day Air (Mail + $5.00)   ☐ Next Day Air (Mail + $15.00)

METHOD OF PAYMENT:
☐ Check or M.O. Payable to Hohm Press, P.O. Box 2501, Prescott, AZ 86302
☐ Call 1-800-381-2700 to place ;your credit card order
☐ Or call 1-928-717-1779 to fax your credit card order
☐ Information for Visa/MasterCard/American Express order only:
   Card# _____ - _____ - _____ - _____ Exp. date: _____

To Receive a Full Catalog, or to Order: 800-381-2700
Visit our website at: www.hohmpress.com or use the accompanying Order Form

ABOUT THE AUTHOR

Born in 1959, Gilles Farcet, Ph.D., is the author of sixteen books and numerous articles. He worked for many years in Paris as a lecturer, journalist, editor, and producer for the French National Radio. Since 1982 he has been a student of Arnaud Desjardins, probably the most famous and respected spiritual guide alive in the French-speaking world today. Gilles started teaching at his master's ashram, Hauteville, in the south of France in 1996.

He is married and the father of two children.

* * *

Additional Information

Several books by Arnaud Desjardins have been translated into English and are available through Hohm Press. See the Recommended Reading section in this book.

To contact Gilles Farcet, write c/o Hohm Press, P.O. Box 2501, Prescott, Arizona, 86302, U.S.A.